A FEW RED DROPS

A FEW RED DROPS

THE CHICAGO RACE RIOT OF 1919

CLAIRE HARTFIELD

CLARION BOOKS
Houghton Mifflin Harcourt
Boston • New York

*Overleaf: Chicago
Skyline, night view,
ca. 1920s.*

Clarion Books
3 Park Avenue
New York, New York 10016

Copyright © 2018 by Claire Hartfield

Clarion Books is an imprint of Houghton Mifflin Harcourt Publishing Company.

www.hmhco.com

The text was set in Mrs Eaves OT.

Library of Congress Cataloging-in-Publication Data is available.
ISBN 978-0-544-78513-7
PRINTED IN THE UNITED STATES OF AMERICA
DOW 10 9 8 7 6 5 4 3
4500754412

To Emily, Caroline, Corinne—and the generations
of young people who will shape the future.

Sometimes I growl, shake myself and
spatter a few red drops for history
to remember. Then—I forget.

—Carl Sandburg
"I Am the People, the Mob"

CONTENTS

*Overleaf: Aerial view of
a Chicago beach.*

ONE
THE BEACH

THE DATE WAS JULY 27, 1919, a day that would forever change the life of John Turner Harris and cause the whole city of Chicago to rethink where it had been and where it was headed.

As is often the case just before catastrophe strikes, that Chicago summer Sunday morning was like any other, carrying no hint of the trouble ahead. Except that it was hot, the unbearable humid kind of hot that sits heavy on the chest and covers the skin with a glistening film of sweat before the day has a chance to get started. The air in fourteen-year-old John's bedroom in his family's home in the city's "Black Belt" was thick with the smell of animal blood that drifted east from the city's stockyards a few miles away. By the height of the day, temperatures would soar to ninety-six degrees—fourteen degrees above normal. And this heat had been building for days.

Those Chicagoans lucky enough to be able to afford the latest technology had electric fans to keep them cool. Those who could not afford such fancy appliances threw windows open to catch the breeze. And still, on this Sunday, the heat turned apartments and houses throughout the city into gigantic ovens. The only escape was to go outside.

♦♦ KEEP

There's room for 250,000 like these at Chicago's Beaches Today

PHOTOGRAPHS BY TRIBUNE
NEWS PHOTO SERVICE

MISS BERNICE
HENNEBERRY (left) and
MISS ANN GLEESON,
Fifty-first Street Beach

MISS RUTH MORINE,
MISS GERTRUDE OHLIN
and MISS CLEONA NELSON,
Winona Beach

MISS
WINIFRED
O'DONNELL,
Wilson Beach

MISS
HELEN
LAGSTROM,
Hollywood
Beach

MISS LOUISE STU...
North Shore Beac...

COOL ! ◆

JAC COUR
and
MARGIE
SCANLON,
Clarendon
Beach

MISS VIVIAN
BOLLING,
Wilson Beach

MISS VIRGINIA
LANE,
Clarendon Beach

ELSIE
DICHTER,
Pearl Beach

MISS DOROTHY CLARKE
(left) and
MISS FRIEDA GLICK,
Winona Beach

*During the heat wave,
Chicagoans were advised
to cool off at the beach.*

TWO

A TIME TO REAP

John and his friends dashed back to the Twenty-Sixth Street beach and poured out their anger to the black bathers there. Around fifty men sprinted down to Twenty-Ninth Street to see for themselves what was going on.

Watching the bathers storm down the beach, John began to think about himself and the trouble he might be in. His mother would be furious if she found out he had been swimming on a Sunday. John later remembered how upset he was: "I wasn't going home because I knew I had better cool myself down." Maybe if he left the scene, she would never know he had been there. He gathered the remaining Williams boys and boarded the first bus that appeared. They traveled nearly four miles south to the Fifty-Fifth Street beach, where they left the bus and sat unnoticed, trying to calm down.

The boys were preoccupied with avoiding punishment at home. But whether they knew it or not, if someone identified them, they could be swept up in deeper trouble than that. Racial confrontation was big news, the kind of news that made headlines

"The Color Line Has Reached the North": An editorial cartoon in the Chicago Tribune *on July 28, 1919, referenced Chicago's racial tension.*

in the *Chicago Defender* and would be read by the thousands of black subscribers in Chicago and around the nation. Police might start poking around, looking for someone black to take the fall. As it turned out, the news was much bigger than the boys could ever have imagined. Back at the Twenty-Ninth Street beach, the anger was gathering momentum that would wreak havoc far beyond Eugene's death, spattering blood across the city. As the *Defender* observed, the rage didn't blow in out of nowhere that day on the beach: "For years [America] has been sowing the wind and now she is reaping the whirlwind."

PART TWO

FIRST WHISPERS

The power which resides in him is new in nature,
and none but he knows what that is which he can
do, nor does he know until he has tried.

—Ralph Waldo Emerson,
"Self-Reliance"

THREE
FREEDOM FIGHT

EUGENE WILLIAMS'S MOTHER BURIED her son a few days later, some seventeen years after she had brought him into the world one spring day in Georgia. When the family moved up north, Eugene had found that some of the other children at his school had roots in New York or Philadelphia or had been born right there in Chicago. But most of the kids, or their parents, grandparents, or great-grandparents, had started out life in the South.

In Chicago's first days, in the middle decades of the 1800s, when slavery was the law of the South, a handful of blacks, almost too small in number to be noticed, came to northern country looking for freedom. Born slave or born free, most could tell a tale of escape.

One southerner, named John Jones, came to get away from becoming part of an inheritance. He had been born free—one of the lucky ones—to a black mother and a white father in North Carolina. Jones was solidly built and, when he reached adulthood, sported a pair of curly sideburns that covered most of his cheeks. His mother, wanting the best for him, sent him off to learn a trade in Tennessee under the watchful eye of a white tailor there. While in Tennessee, Jones met the Richardsons, a free black family who warmly took him into their social world. But Mr. Richardson grew restless with the rules constricting black life in Memphis and moved the family, including daughter Mary, whom Jones had come to love, up to free country in Alton, Illinois.

Left behind and lonely, Jones suffered more bad news. The tailor he worked for became deathly ill, and word had it that his heirs were planning to claim Jones as bequeathed to them under the tailor's will and sell him into slavery. Jones was not one to lie down paralyzed by the specter of danger. Before the law could declare him to be just another piece of property subject to disposal as the tailor's heirs saw fit, Jones applied to the courts for protec-

John Jones. Portrait by Aaron E. Darling, ca. 1865.

tion and obtained a certificate of freedom. He stayed in the South and worked for a few years to save some money, then packed up, headed to Illinois, and proposed to Mary Richardson, the love of his life. In 1845, married and caring for a newborn daughter, John and Mary decided to move farther north and make Chicago their home.

Even in free Illinois, the road was not without danger. John and Mary were stopped along the way, seemingly for no reason other than the color of their skin. A sheriff demanded their freedom papers, looked them over, detained the couple still, clearly unsatisfied, searching for a reason to send them back south. Then the white stagecoach driver put in a good word on their behalf and the sheriff begrudgingly let them continue on their way. But the Joneses knew there were more sheriffs lurking in towns throughout Illinois and across the northern states. A white man in Chicago, L. C. Freer, who would later become the Joneses' friend and ally, affirmed the truth the Joneses were experiencing: Some blacks might be free, "but they were looked upon as beings who had no right to exist outside of slavery, by a very large part of the community."

When the Joneses reached Chicago, they befriended a group of abolitionists, black and white, working together as "conductors," assisting slaves to freedom on the hidden tracks of the Underground Railroad. John and Mary and the other abolitionists opened their homes and offices as "depots," always prepared for a middle-of-the-night knock on the door, then shadowed brown figures emerging from under straw piled high on a horse-drawn wagon and slipping silently into the warm refuge offered to them. Mary remembered an abolitionist assuring stowaways, "'Mrs. Jones will take good care of you to-day,' and of course I said 'Yes.'"

The first city census in 1837 put the number of blacks at 77 out of 4,066 residents, though the number of blacks fluctuated from time to time—increasing some when a few new slaves arrived safe from the South, decreasing again when Canada beckoned and Chicago didn't seem quite far enough north to guarantee safety, or when slave catchers proved those fears right on target, waving the Fugitive Slave Act as legal authority to nab blacks off the streets and drag them back into bondage.

Those who stayed in Chicago, setting up house and looking for work, found that only the lowest jobs were open to blacks. Most labored as maids and waiters in homes and hotels, making just enough to get by. A few, the most successful, worked for themselves, running a grocery or a barbershop. John Jones joined them, opening a tailor shop to clean and repair elegant suits and dresses for the wealthy whites in town.

Straight-backed, prim Mary set up a modest but respectable home near the city center, a part of town where blacks and whites lived peaceably together.

Despite the limits on their freedom, blacks took pleasure in this place where they had some measure of control: they could choose a home, earn wages, decide whom to marry, sign up their children for a public education—a mighty bit better than life on the plantation. Lewis Isbel, a black barber who claimed to have shaved the city's first mayor and President Abraham Lincoln, talked about his work with pride. As recalled by one of his contemporaries, Isbel was "content with the reflected greatness which shone on the blade of his razor and now settled on him."

Still, Illinois had Black Laws that made sure blacks like the Joneses and Isbel understood the reality: They might be free, but they were not equal. They were not allowed to vote, to sit on a jury, or to testify against a white man in court. It seemed particularly unfair to them that white immigrants new to America, born in foreign lands, could vote and could find higher-paying jobs in manufacturing industries—rights that native-born blacks were denied.

Printed at the   "TELEGRAPH"—ALTON.

UNITED STATES OF AMERICA,

STATE OF ILLINOIS,
Madison County, } ss. { To all to whom these Presents may come—GREETING:

𝕶𝖓𝖔𝖜 𝖄𝖊, That *John Jones*

a person of Color, about *twenty seven* year of age, *post five*

feet *six* inches high, *Mulatto*

complexion,

has exhibited, presented and filed, in the Office of the Clerk of the Circuit Court of the County and State aforesaid, a 𝕮𝕰𝕽𝕿𝕴𝕱𝕴𝕮𝕬𝕿𝕰, duly authen= ticated, of **FREEDOM,** as such person of Color, *has a Scarr over the Left Eye Brow a Scratch across his cheek and a Scarr on the Left Shin bone Taylor to Trate*

Now, therefore, I, **WM. TYLER BROWN,** Clerk of the Circuit Court of Madison County, State of Illinois, 𝕮𝕰𝕽𝕿𝕴𝕱𝖄, That said *John Jones* is a FREE PERSON OF COLOR, a resi= dent or citizen of the State of Illinois, and entitled to be respected accord= ingly, in Person and Property, at all times and places, in the due prosecu= tion of *his* Lawful concerns.

In Testimony whereof, I have, to these Presents, signed my name, and affixed the Seal of said Court, at Edwardsville, this 2 8th day of *November* in the year of our Lord one thousand eight hundred and forty=four

Wm T Brown Clerk.

John Jones's certificate of freedom.

In 1850, the lives of blacks got harder. A new law roped every citizen of the United States into conspiracy with the slave catchers, requiring everyone to search out and turn in any slaves they knew to be in hiding.

The Joneses' white abolitionist friends were outraged. Chicago's governing council rebelled, issuing its own public resolution that defied the new law as "revolting to our moral sense" and telling Chicagoans, "We do not therefore consider it a part of our duty . . . to aid or assist in the arrest of fugitives from oppression."

John and Mary Jones and their fellow black Chicagoans were beyond angry—they had much more at stake than their principles. Now subject to the new law and alert to potential trouble, they could not help but scan their surroundings as they walked to work or made a quick trip to the grocery store or simply stepped out for a sunny Sunday stroll. At any given moment, their freedom could be challenged.

Mary Richardson Jones, ca. 1865.

founding fathers, William B. Ogden, argued strenuously for expatriation—sending the freed slaves far, far away to countries in Central and South America.

Nonetheless, the streams of fleeing slaves became rivers of newly freed southern blacks entering Chicago each day. In 1870, nearly 3,700 blacks called the city their home.

The end of slavery broke the dam, and the rights of citizenship began to roll in. In early 1865, Illinois struck down its Black Laws and became the first state to ratify the Thirteenth Amendment, which enshrined in the Constitution the end of slavery. Three years later, the Fourteenth Amendment granted blacks full citizenship. Another two years on, the Fifteenth Amendment extended to black men the right to vote. Jones organized his people into the Republican Party, the party of Abraham Lincoln, which Jones referred to as the "great party of freedom," to make them a political force. In 1871, John Jones became the first black Chicagoan elected to political office. By the time he died, eight years later, the next generation of black leaders was hard at work, eager to claim for their people the bounty of that freedom John Jones had spent his life fighting for.

FOUR

SELF-RELIANCE

WHEN BLACKS GOT CLOSE UP on it, the gleam of full citizenship failed to shine as brightly as they had hoped. They began the 1870s with optimism, buoyed by their new constitutional rights. But through the end of the nineteenth century and into the beginning of the twentieth, black men and women setting out to work where they wanted, live where they wanted, and play where they wanted found that most white employers, apartment owners, and restaurant hostesses firmly turned them away.

Whites who had fought so valiantly for the end of slavery now focused on their self-interest, patching things up with white southerners and courting northern businessmen. Blacks would have to do for themselves. Ferdinand Barnett was among those determined to lead his people toward equality. He had been born in the South in 1858 to a slave father and a free mother. During the Civil War, the Barnett family fled to free Canada, then resettled in Chicago when the end of slavery made it safe. Barnett excelled, attending Northwestern University and opening his own law office right there in Chicago when he was just twenty years old. As he walked past the rundown homes in the black neighborhood where many of his people now lived, and heard stories of "No Negroes Need Apply," it was clear to Barnett that the engine of progress had stalled for most blacks. He felt compelled to take a stand. In 1878, he started Chicago's first black newspaper, the *Conservator,* and called blacks to action: "We are no longer slaves. We intend to act the part of free men."

Like Barnett, Ida B. Wells started out with optimism for a bright future. Born in Holly Springs, Mississippi, Wells was just one year old when she was freed from slavery. She grew up with a fierce will to help her people move successfully into the new day. Her plan was to stay in her native South, teaching school and writing for the local newspaper, because she believed that "the people

Ferdinand Barnett.

who had little or no school training should have something coming into their homes weekly which dealt with their problems in a simple, helpful way."

Her articles were a hit, reprinted in other papers, making a name for Ida as "Princess of the Press." As she later remembered, for a time she was "happy in the thought that our influence was helpful and that I was doing the work I loved and had proved that I could make a living out of it." But in 1892, when Wells was thirty years old, her world was shattered. One of her closest friends, the father of her godchild, was lynched. Along with two other men, he was seized and brutally murdered by a mob of white men. Ida recalled, "The lynching . . . changed the whole course of my life."

Wells's stories now turned to exposing the gruesome wave of murder rolling across the South—as Ida called it, "an excuse to get rid of Negroes who were acquiring wealth and property." This tide of hate threatened to roll right over Ida. While she was on a trip to New York, a group of leading citizens back home ransacked her print shop and left a note warning that her return to the paper would be "punished with death." This was enough to keep Wells away, but she was not to be shut down. As one of her admirers observed, "She has plenty of nerve and is as sharp as a steel trap." She moved her base up north and continued speaking out in cities around the country. "I, too," she said, "could tell of much segregation that was going on in the North—in school, in church, in hotels, to say nothing of social affairs."

On a trip to Chicago in 1893, short, round fireball Ida Wells got to know tall, debonair, easygoing Ferdinand Barnett as they worked together on a pamphlet calling out racial inequities. They became admirers of each other's passion for justice, and then they found a deeper connection, fell in love, and got married. The whole of Chicago's black community and a few white friends turned out to celebrate. "The interest of the public in the affair," Ida recalled, "seemed to be so great that not only the church filled

Ida Wells-Barnett.

to overflowing, but the streets surrounding the church were so packed with humanity that it was almost impossible for the carriage bearing the bridal party to reach the church door." The two became joined, as family and as leaders, in what Ferdinand called the "continued warfare for our rights." They worked with other leaders nationally, but their home was in Chicago's black community, which, by their fifth wedding anniversary, in 1900, was over 30,000 strong.

The Barnetts belonged to a small elite group referred to by the esteemed black sociologist St. Clair Drake as "the Refined." These men and women were college educated and had careers as lawyers, doctors, journalists, businesspeople, and politicians. But they amounted to only a tiny fraction of Chicago's blacks, and their ranks were slow to grow.

At the other end of the economic scale was a small group of ne'er-do-wells whom Drake called "the Riffraff." These were the penny-ante gamblers, the prostitutes, the petty criminals, who could be found, day or night, playing the numbers in poolrooms, drinking in bars, or roaming the streets, looking for trouble. They shared their part of town with the group referred to by another black historian as the "Economically Dispossessed"—freed slaves and Civil War veterans who eked out the barest of livings on sporadic day labor or fell back on the charitable donations of the more fortunate in their community.

By far the largest group of blacks was working class, a layer of society Drake sometimes referred to as "the Respectables." Though the Respectables had steady work, their wages were consistently low, as they found themselves shut out of higher-paying factory jobs in Chicago's fast-growing industrial base. Black men worked as butlers in the homes of the rich, shining shoes, polishing silverware, serving guests at parties. Or they took up positions in the glitzy new downtown hotels and restaurants, waiting on tables and cleaning floors. The luckiest ones worked for the post office or as porters on the railroads. Many black women among the Respectables were also up and out of the house early, serving as maids or laundresses all day, then returning home to cook and clean for their husbands and children before dropping into bed.

Searching for a way to get ahead, some blacks stuck in service jobs thought that joining forces in an organized way, black and white laborers together, might be their ticket to something better. The hundreds of black men working as waiters were tired of putting in long hours for little pay. One on one, the lowly worker was no match for the powerful restaurant owner who could fire and replace him in an instant. Black waiters were cautiously optimistic that by banding together with white waiters, they might bring their employers to the bargaining table.

In 1890, Chicago's black waiters joined the German-led Culinary Alliance and walked out on strike. Ferdinand Barnett did what he could to aid the strikers, publishing an open letter in a Chicago newspaper to rouse community support. The waiters stood strong. And it worked. Soon blacks were gathered at Quinn Chapel, celebrating the first-ever wage scale in Chicago that gave equal pay to black and white waiters. Enthusiasm for the union was sky-high.

A server waits for a man's teacup.

A little more than a decade later, the rosy picture was fraying around the edges. On the first Monday in May 1903, black waiters arrived to begin work at a popular lunch counter only to be told to go home, as the manager had abruptly declared them "incompetent." White waitresses were standing by, ready to take their place. Once again, white and black waiters went out on strike together. But this time, in the settlement that followed, black rights to equal wages were left on the cutting-room floor. It was a stinging slap to all of the black workers who had hitched their fortunes to the white man's union. White restaurant owners followed up with the knockout punch of firing black men and replacing them with white women. It was a lesson blacks would not forget.

While the Respectables were putting most of their energies into making ends meet, the Refined were mapping out plans to make the heart of the black residential area a vibrant place to live. Huddling at their exclusive clubs, the patriarchs steered construction of important institutions to serve their black brothers and sisters. The Colored Men's Library Association was built in 1887, a gathering place for black men to read and listen to lectures. Provident Hospital and nursing school for black women opened in 1891, providing high-quality medical care for the growing black community. The new facility included black doctors and nurses on staff at a time when many white hospitals turned them away. In 1914, the five-story redbrick Young Men's Christian Association on the south end of Wabash Avenue welcomed blacks who were turned away by whites at the YMCA downtown. Donations from wealthy white businessmen were essential to getting these projects off the ground, but the guiding force was the black elite.

The ladies of the Refined led their own efforts to fill their community's needs. In 1893, Ida Wells-Barnett launched the first black women's club in Chicago, recruiting an aging Mary Richardson Jones to join as honorary chairperson. The Ida B. Wells Club served as a model for the organization of the city's black women who had time to spare. Some engaged primarily in planning parties and charity balls. Others took up the mantle of "social motherhood," focused on care of black children and the poor.

In 1896, Ida Wells-Barnett became a mother herself. Shortly after that, she resigned from her job as a journalist, finding that "the duties of wife and mother were a profession in themselves." But she remained a force in the community until her death more than three decades later. To jump-start the youngest children into a better life, she sponsored a kindergarten. Moved, as she recounted, by "the story of numbers of unfortunate young men [she] had visited at the Joliet prison," she opened the Negro Fellowship League, calling it "an ounce of prevention" to save as many as she could from the tragedy of the streets. She provided the safe space of a reading room on the first floor, low-rent lodging upstairs, and an employment bureau to provide leads on jobs.

Blacks also exercised their recently gained voting rights to boost their fortunes. In John Jones's day, before blacks could vote, they had cast their lot with Republicans, their best hope for freedom. But in Ferdinand and Ida's day, blacks did not feel bound to vote along party lines, and did not hesitate to get behind any candidate—Republican or Democrat—who was most likely to support their people. It was no surprise that, in 1900, the black patriarchs organized their community in support of a Democratic mayor who included them when passing out jobs and a Republican alderman who funded improvements, including the black community's first neighborhood playground.

Men were not the only ones to recognize the power of the ballot. In 1913, though women had not yet achieved the right to vote in federal elections, Illinois extended local suffrage to women. Ida Wells-Barnett organized the Alpha Suffrage Club to conduct door-to-door registration and sign up legions of new women voters. This raised some eyebrows among men of the black community, but there was no arguing with success. Adding women voters made the black vote a force to be reckoned with, and important candidates came to call. Like her husband, Ida preached neither Democrat nor Republican but encouraged blacks to "vote for the advantage of ourselves and our race."

In the late 1800s and early 1900s, the Barnetts worked not just for Chicago but for black America. Ferdinand or Ida or both were often to be found planning strategy or making speeches in churches, associations, and political backrooms. Ferdinand was tapped by President William McKinley to lead a campaign to re-energize black enthusiasm for the Republican Party. Ida helped found the National Association for the Advancement of Colored People (NAACP) to take up her anti-lynching campaign alongside issues of poverty, politics, and power.

Chicago's black community moved slowly toward equality. But even as progress was made, new challenges loomed around every corner. As Ida Wells-Barnett cautioned, it was necessary to be as "alert as the watchman on the wall."

FIVE
WHITE NEGROES

Just west of Chicago's Black Belt sat the white immigrant communities known as Packingtown. The men and women who settled there had come to get away from oppression in their homeland. Irish and Germans arrived in the mid-nineteenth century, Poles and Lithuanians a few decades later.

They came with dreams of a better tomorrow. But for many, life did not turn out as they hoped. In 1919, while young Packingtown toughs roamed the South Side heckling blacks, their mothers and fathers toiled long hours in the nearby Union Stock Yard, earning the barest living by slaughtering and packaging hundreds of thousands of pigs, sheep, and cows each day. As one policeman put it, Packingtown was a "pretty tough hole."

———— ❦ ————

Packingtown had grown over the last half of the nineteenth century as part of a massive transformation in the way America's meat was processed. Up until the mid-1800s, livestock was slaughtered on small farms and the meat was sold locally in towns that dotted the countryside. By the early 1900s, meatpacking had centralized: nearly 90 percent of all beef inspected east of the Rocky Mountains was processed by six big companies. These meatpacking giants were headquartered in Chicago.

The consolidation of the industry started with innovations in transportation: first canals, then railroads. Chicago, incorporated in 1837, was at the center of both, for one reason: location. In the 1830s and '40s, the Illinois and Michigan Canal was built to connect a chain of waterways from the Mississippi River in the west to the Hudson River in the east, with Chicago sitting smack-dab in the middle.

By 1848, the year the canal was completed, the nation's attention had turned to building railroads. Steam locomotives could go anywhere tracks could be laid: over mountains and through forests. They would keep chugging in winter, when canal traffic was immobilized by ice. They would blow past canal boats with unparalleled speed. In the space of ten years, new railroad lines were laid, track by track, four thousand miles, sprawling east, west, south, and north from the central terminus: Chicago.

Laboring men were needed to dig the canal and lay the tracks. Irish immigrants answered the call. The work was backbreaking: digging out boulders, chopping down trees, dynamiting tunnels, and hammering in railroad ties. Many men were crushed, drowned, blown up, or laid low by toxic water, to the point where there was said to be "an Irishman buried under every [railroad] tie."

In the old country, they had toiled as tenant farmers under the oppressive control of their English landlords. The English Protestants thoroughly detested the Irish Catholics. One immigrant recalled, "Our immediate ancestors, fathers and grandfathers, felt the iron heel upon their necks in their early lives, and in our childhood we were fed with stories of eviction, landlord oppressions, and religious persecutions which sent us to bed night after night in fear and trembling lest before morning some Englishman should get into the house and snatch the children away in chains and slavery."

The worst bore down upon the Irish in the 1840s, when the potato crop, their food of life, rotted in the ground for four years running, and landlords heartlessly threw their tenants into the streets. One million Irish Catholics died; another million and a half fled into the arms of America. As one woman declared, "There's a curse on ould green Ireland and we'll get out of it."

Arriving in the United States, the Irish found that life in the new country was not much better. American white Protestants treated them like scum. The same Irishman who recalled oppression in the homeland observed, "We saw in it all, translated to this side of the Atlantic, the same spirit of persecution which drove our fathers from the land of their birth, and we have come to manhood carrying chips on our shoulders because of the things which men have done to us on account of our race and religion."

On the job, slurs and slights were an everyday experience. One Irishman observed bitterly: "The colleens who found jobs in the kitchens of the wealthy were called 'pot-wallopers,' 'biddies,' and 'kitchen canaries.'" The men hired as laborers were called "'greenhorns,' 'clodhoppers,' 'Micks,' or 'Paddies.'" And those were the lucky ones. Many searching for work were turned away by postings stating "No Irish Need Apply."

Much to the dismay of the Irish, sometimes white America lumped them together with blacks, referring to them as "white negroes" and to blacks as "smoked Irish." A tongue-in-cheek story made the rounds, in which a black man complained, "My master is a great tyrant. He treats me as badly as if I was a common Irishman."

Chicago was a hotbed of prejudice. Opening the local paper, it was not uncommon for an Irishman to find himself the subject of scathing commentary, such as one journalist's characterization of the Irish as "the most depraved, debased, worthless and irredeemable drunkards and sots which curse the community."

SIX

WASTE MATTERS

IN THE EARLY 1880s, Irishman John T. Joyce was a thriving member of the Packingtown community. Young and bursting with cocky energy, Joyce worked as a cattle butcher. He could "dress" a cow from start to finish: skin it, split its bones, gut it, and cut the meat into pieces. The work took tremendous strength and dexterity. Joyce bragged that the butchers "had a highly skilled trade and were high priced men."

The butchers identified with one another as a brotherhood. Joyce commented: "It was wonderful to see the good fellowship existing between those cattle butchers. No matter where they came from, it was only necessary to be a cattle butcher."

At the end of every day, the butchers lovingly cleaned and stored their knives and cleavers, the tools of their trade. At summer socials, their day of fun was capped off with the ultimate celebration of a butcher's skill—the cattle-dressing contest. The best, who were fabled heroes, were able to cut up a steer in under five minutes. At the end of life, a fallen brother was honored by his fellow butchers with a last tribute: an elaborate funeral wreath in the shape of a broken cleaver.

John Joyce worked for Swift & Company, named after its founder, Gustavus Franklin Swift, a man who demanded and respected excellence. Like Joyce, Swift had learned the butchering process from start to finish, entering the trade as his brother's apprentice in 1855 at the age of fourteen in a little town on Cape Cod. But Swift's interests went far beyond the butchering process. As his son later said about him, "Gustavus Franklin Swift was never content simply to get on. Always he saw opportunities ahead." He wanted to build something spectacular.

At sixteen, Gustavus, who went by the name G.F., set his sights on the big city of Boston. But the Swift family had deep roots in Cape Cod going back 250 years, and G.F.'s father did not want him to leave the family home. To entice him to stay, G.F.'s father offered him twenty-five dollars to set up his own business right there on Cape Cod, a challenge and an opportunity that G.F. agreed to take on.

He bought his first cow for nineteen dollars, sold her meat for twenty-nine dollars, bought more cows, sold more meat, increasing his profits cow by cow, until he had enough money to open his own shop, buy more cows, sell more meat, open a second and then a third shop. He worked sixteen-hour days with a tireless energy. His thoughts on this subject were abundantly clear: "When a clerk says he must leave the office because it is five o'clock, you'll never see his name over a front door."

Cape Cod was an adequate place for Swift to start. But it was too small for him to stay in. He moved his business to larger towns, first in Massachusetts, then in New York State, always looking for the best market. Swift knew that Chicago's Union Stock Yard, opened in 1865, was the largest in the world. He realized that if he was to build something extraordinary, he must make Chicago his home.

Gustavus Franklin Swift.

Swift arrived in Chicago in 1875 and set up shop. At that time, the Union Stock Yard was dominated by two other meat men: Philip Armour, who specialized in pork; and Nelson Morris, who dealt principally in beef. Swift quickly established himself as a third power in the Stock Yard. Together Armour, Morris, and Swift became known as the "Big Three."

Swift's guiding principle for success was simple and constant: eliminate waste to increase profits. As his son later observed, "To my father any waste was too much!"

First problem: how to preserve fresh meat dressed in Chicago so that it could be shipped without spoilage to customers in far-away cities and towns. Solution: the development of a refrigerated railcar. Before Swift's investment in this groundbreaking innovation, there was no way to keep meat fresh long enough to transport it long distances. Most livestock was shipped live to be butchered in branch houses located near the households where the meat would be cooked and eaten. Chicago companies slaughtered and packaged only enough meat to satisfy the needs of local residents. With the development of the refrigerated car in the late 1870s, meat dressed in Chicago could be shipped to the many people living in New York, Boston, and other East Coast cities. The number of cows slaughtered in Chicago grew from a quarter million in 1875 to two and a quarter million in 1890.

Next problem: finding uses for all the animal parts that were ending up on the scrap heap. Solution: turning bones into knife handles, blood into fertilizer, beef fat into margarine. By 1903, fully 25 percent of the "Big Three" meatpacking companies' profit on beef came from their ingenious ways of using what had formerly been thrown away. Gustavus Swift boasted about the clever use of animal byproducts: "Now we use all of the hog except his grunt."

Third problem: how to increase speed on the job. Solution: investment in machinery that moved slaughtered livestock from one place to the next, eliminating slowdowns. Before the use of hoists and conveyors, cows were moved through the various stages of slaughter by hand. For example, stunned cows, each weighing nearly a ton, would simply fall to the floor and have to be dragged by three or four men to be hung up for slicing open and skinning. Machines eliminated this waste of time and manpower.

Swift had one more problem: his butcher workmen. Swift admired the talents of his butchers, some of whom were more skilled than Swift himself. He made a point of remembering at promotion time "a man worth keeping an eye on." But as Swift saw it, high pay was waste, a problem to be solved. He thought things through. Many parts of the butchering process did not require the skill of Johnny Joyce and the other butcher aristocrats. Maybe, Swift thought, he could separate out the gut-grabbing, the kidney-pulling, and the tail-ripping and give these tasks to unskilled men at dirt-cheap, unskilled wages.

Swift knew there were blacks wandering the streets and docks looking for work. Even those employed as waiters and janitors might be enticed to leave personal service for the higher wages of the stockyards. But Swift was interested in a different solution. As the nineteenth century drew to a close, he saw a massive new wave of men flooding into Chicago, fleeing oppression in eastern Europe—from Poland, Czechoslovakia, Lithuania.

Swift knew that these men would be hungry for unskilled jobs in the Yard. With that in mind, he divided the butcher's job into close to a hundred different parts, and handed out those parts to more than a hundred different men.

Men inspect hanging cattle carcasses.

In 1901, Anatanas Kaztauskis came to Chicago from Lithuania, eager to take on the unskilled work that Swift had created. His aunt had sent word ahead from Lithuania to friends who agreed to provide Kaztauskis with lodging. As he made his way across Chicago's Packingtown to the boarding house where he was to stay, he passed people in the street talking in many different languages: English spoken in Irish brogue, German, Polish, Czech, Italian. But as he drew nearer to the address he had been given, the other languages fell away and the familiar lilt of the Lithuanian tongue enveloped him. Finally arrived, he was shown to the basement of a small boarding house, where he was to share sleeping space on the floor with three other boarders.

The next night, the men in the house took Kaztauskis out to see the city. He was amazed: "We walked all around a store that filled one whole block and had walls of glass. . . . We saw shiny carriages and automobiles. I saw men with dress suits, I saw women with such clothes that I could not think at all." The glamour reminded Kaztauskis of how little he had: "I felt poor and my shoes got very bad." As the men walked back home, Kaztauskis looked down at the river. "It was so full of grease and dirt and sticks and boxes," he thought, "that it looked like a big, wide, dirty street, except in some places, where it boiled up. It made me sick to look at it." That night, he could not fall asleep for a long time.

He was up at five o'clock the next morning, closing the boarding house door behind him, joining thousands of immigrant men and women making their way through the streets toward the Union Stock Yard. Ahead of him towered the Yard's great gate, a wide center arch flanked on either side by ornately carved turrets and two smaller gates. A carved stone bull's head sat high above the center arch, gazing down at the stream of humanity that passed below it.

The Great Gate of the Union Stock Yard.

Inside the Yard, the apparatus of the world's largest meatpacking facility sprawled over three hundred acres: animal pens large enough to hold 75,000 cattle, 300,000 hogs and 105,000 sheep; a horse exchange amphitheater; a sales pavilion; four hundred business offices; the National Live Stock Bank; and the three-hundred-room Transit House hotel. Each of the Big Three meatpacking company owners claimed a large corner of the Yard for his company's facilities. Smaller packinghouses were scattered throughout the premises.

That first day, Kaztauskis walked to the entrance of one of the meatpacking plants, joining a crowd of about two hundred hungry-looking men standing outside for the morning "shape-up." A man in uniform opened the slaughterhouse door and stepped out, looked the men over, then pointed his finger—you, you, you. Twenty-three men in all followed him into the packinghouse. The rest remained outside, watching the door close on any chance at work for the day. Kaztauskis later remembered, "One boy sat down and cried, just next to me, on a pile of boards. Some policemen waved their clubs and we all walked on."

Men were now trudging away from the shapeups at the other slaughterhouses, looking dejected and hopeless. Kaztauskis met up with other Lithuanians who said they had come to the shapeup every morning for three weeks. Walking away from the Yard, he felt "bad and tired and hungry." That night, a man let Kaztauskis in on a little secret to success. Before the next shapeup, Kaztauskis slipped five dollars to the uniformed man, and this time, as he stood with the others hoping to be chosen, the uniformed man pointed at him.

Now Anatanas joined more than a hundred and fifty men working on the cattle-killing floor. Overhead conveyors carried livestock down a "disassembly" line. First the knocker dealt each cow a blow to the head. Then the shackler cuffed its hind foot and the animal was machine-lifted to the sticker, who ended the animal's life with a cut to the throat. The cow then moved down a long row of workmen—the skinner, the backer, the rumper, and so on—each doing his own small part to turn cows into steaks and roasts and prepare them for shipping to dinner tables across the country. Several decades later, borrowing from this technology, Henry Ford credited the meatpackers for the idea that led to the invention of the automobile assembly line.

His first day on the job, Kaztauskis worked from six in the morning until seven in the evening and the next day from six to eight. His job was to push into a drain the gallons of animal blood that spilled out along the floor. The room was hot. The blood was hot. The foreman, whose pay depended on speed, walked up and down the line, pushing the men to work faster, faster. Or, as one packinghouse manager explained, "If you need to turn out a little

more, you speed up the conveyors a little and the men speed up to keep pace." One of Kaztauskis's fellow workers had a different way of looking at it: "They get all the blood out of those cattle and all the work out of us men."

<hr>

Gustavus Swift was pleased. With so much unskilled labor looking for work, he was no longer dependent on Johnny Joyce and his skilled butchers. But there were still a few tasks that required the skills of the master butcher. In recognition of this, Swift and his fellow meatpacking company owners kept them on as part of the expanded work force and even paid them at a higher rate than the unskilled men. But the skilled butchers were now a small part of a huge, mostly unskilled labor pool. The bosses controlled everything: hours, pace, and wages. Problem solved. As Chicago moved into the twentieth century, the golden days for Joyce and the other butcher aristocrats were over.

SEVEN

PARALLEL UNIVERSES

AT THE BEGINNING OF THE TWENTIETH CENTURY, the immigrants who worked for Swift and his fellow meatpackers lived in a group of neighborhoods that sat in a U shape surrounding the Union Stock Yard, together referred to as Packingtown. Blacks, most of whom did not work for Swift, coalesced in the narrow strip of land just east of the immigrants, forming the community that came to be known as the Black Belt.

Middle- and upper-class whites were happy to keep poor white immigrants out of sight, out of mind. One outsider said of the population: "Packingtown begins to seem like a little world in itself. You feel that here is a great mass of humanity, the kind that is hardest to manage, the easiest to inflame, the slowest to understand." As for blacks, most whites preferred that all of them—the Barnetts and their fellow Refined as well as poorer folks—stayed among their own.

The western boundary of the Black Belt met the eastern boundary of Packingtown at Wentworth Avenue, presenting the opportunity for all sorts of cooperative interaction between the races: in stores, schools, parks, each other's homes. Instead, the immigrants declared the border to be a "deadline" and treated any black person crossing over as an invader of their turf. Two worlds developed side by side, wholly separate.

The world of Packingtown was tough and poor, a collection of shanties and shops in the shadow of the Yard. The chimneys of Swift's packing plant stood tall against the sky, belching thick smoke that spread over Packingtown like a blanket, smothering the community below in the stench of blood.

Most immigrant families successful enough to afford better—the doctors, lawyers, and businessmen—packed up and resettled in middle-class communities, usually with other families from the homeland.

Most of those who worked in the Yard, including the skilled butchers still employed by Swift and his fellow bosses, chose to stay put in Packingtown, a short walk from work. The quick commute was one of the small graces they could appreciate, as it gave them just that little bit of extra time after the quitting horn sounded. It also saved the pennies that would otherwise have paid their fare on the streetcar and instead could be used to buy a better cut of meat for Sunday dinner. Most important, it allowed them to get to work on a moment's notice, should they suddenly be called up from one of the frequent temporary layoffs.

Foot traffic flowed through the main business arteries of Packingtown at all times of day: men disappearing into and emerging from one of the more than five hundred saloons on "Whiskey Row"; women visiting the grocer, the shoemaker, and the like; children chasing pigeons or rodents in the streets as they waited for their mothers to finish shopping.

Within the sanctuary of the saloons, white men of all ethnicities—including Irish, Poles, and Lithuanians—talked shop and made deals. The unemployed gathered to commiserate after an unsuccessful morning at the shapeup; the employed gathered on the way home after work, stopping to forget their cares for a little while at the end of a long day.

In the saloons, Democratic Irish "bosses," many of them barkeeps, ruled as kings in their courts. Men of all backgrounds paid visits to these politicos, asking them for favors: to cut through red tape around a citizenship application, for instance, or to grease the wheels for approval of a pushcart license, or to cash their paychecks. In exchange, supplicants pledged their votes, helping the Democratic aldermen who filled the city council to fend off their Republican opponents. Riding to victory on these votes, the Irish politicians filled city jobs—policemen, firemen—with their fellow Irishmen, who in turn watched protectively over the Irish and eastern European communities. And so the cycle continued.

Street scene outside a Packingtown saloon.

Above the streets, the steeples of numerous Catholic churches jutted up across the Packingtown skyline. Each parish served a particular ethnic group. As one observer noted, "The Catholics of Chicago are ministered to in twelve different languages." Mass at St. Bridget was in English, at St. Mary of Perpetual Help in Polish, at Holy Cross in Lithuanian. Each church had its own school and social clubs, affirming and maintaining the ways of the homeland, serving as the anchor for community in the new land. No-nonsense nuns ruled classrooms with an iron hand, passing on to the youngest girls and boys the discipline and knowledge they would need to get ahead in a prejudiced world.

Women were left out of the politics of the saloons and found their own roles as leaders under the watchful eye of the nuns or in the settlement houses that were not run by Catholics but provided much-needed social services and had the welfare of all immigrant families at heart.

The final authority for them all was vested in Chicago's bishop. And, most years, that bishop was Irish, a circumstance that met with the general approval of all ethnicities. As one man remarked about the Irish bishop who led the Catholic church in Chicago from 1880 to 1902: "All are unanimous in proclaiming his wisdom and his fairness to each and every member of the Church."

After a long day out in the world, families returned to their dilapidated homes. Johnny Joyce's Irish compatriots dominated Bridgeport; the poorest crowded into the southern subsection of the neighborhood called Canaryville. Many of the newer immigrants from eastern European countries like Poland and Lithuania were relegated to the ramshackle houses just west of the Union Stock Yard in the neighborhood aptly called Back of the Yards. Bleak as the area was, there was no money for anything better; the low wages paid by Swift and his fellow packers kept the unskilled masses living in squalor.

The cramped interior of an immigrant home.

Men were worn down by the backbreaking grind of their work in the Yard. One longtime butcher described the emotional effects: "Generally when men are keyed up to the highest point of speed and endurance, something gives way and the remainder is characteristic and noticeable in all men who work in this manner. As a rule they are irritable, emotional and very sensitive . . . ever ready to resent an insult."

Fathers were often too tired for much happy interaction with their families. One man lamented, "We punish our children until they become cowards and liars, and then we deplore their heartless ingratitude when we in turn become weak and helpless." A drink with the guys was easier. "The presence of the saloons," one observer commented, "may be largely accounted for by the absence of decent and cheerful home life."

Children of Packingtown.

Men came home across the busy avenues to smaller dirt streets, through yards covered with rubbish, up broken steps, into dark, cramped rooms, usually no more than four rooms all told, shared by parents, several children, and a couple of boarders who were taken in to make ends meet. The day room was usually furnished with a coal-heated stove, dining table, and chairs; the sleeping spaces, many without windows, included beds for family members if they could afford them, pallets lining the floor if they could not. Some people slept with guns under their beds to shoot the rats at night.

With so many people in such close quarters, when one person took sick, the rest fell like dominoes. Many children died of tuberculosis, bronchitis, or diphtheria. By 1909, one of every three babies in Packingtown died before age two.

In these dire circumstances, survival depended on specific, well-defined contributions from each member of the family. The men were the primary providers. In good times, when wages were up, the family might enjoy a little extra mutton on the table or a new pair of shoes. When wages were down or workers were laid off during slow seasons, the family was often not sure where the next meal was coming from.

Few married women worked outside the home, but their days were full of tasks every bit as necessary as their husbands' to keep the family afloat. One female contributor to a journal reporting on issues important to laborers was unsparingly honest about these women: "They get up at 5 o'clock in the morning and never go to bed until 10 or 11 o'clock at night. They work without ceasing the whole of that time. . . . No sacrifice is deemed too great for them to make, and no incompetency in any branch of their work is excused." Caring for the typical seven-person household of two parents, two children, and three boarders, there was oatmeal to boil, meat to roast; a table to set, clear, and clean; dishes to wash; mud- and blood-soaked clothing to scrub, hang to dry, mend, fold; groceries to bargain for; children to manage; sick

A woman carrying wood. Women's chores typically included heavy labor.

patients to nurse; and "off the books" laundry and sewing taken in for a small fee. If time permitted, they might make their way to the local parish or a nearby settlement house to spend an hour sharing neighborhood news with other women. Worn and invisible, summed up by a Packingtown man as "bitter brooding mothers," many women were angry at the world—their husbands, their children, but mostly Swift and his compatriots and anyone else they saw as making their lives more difficult.

Since homes were too cramped for play space, children not in school found themselves shooed outdoors to join pickup play groups or scavenge the nearby dump. There they climbed up mountains of garbage, pulling out items their families might find useful—food, kindling, discarded furniture. The younger ones admired the older boys who strutted about so tough, and they jostled with their playmates for a chance to run errands for the gangs of young men they looked up to.

A pregnant woman rests her heavy sack against a barrel.

By the time they reached fourteen, many young people were pulled out of school and called upon to earn their keep as messenger boys, door openers, office girls, and seamstresses. Although it was understood that their earnings went into the family coffers, many pocketed a portion of their take, boys shelling out for an evening at the movies, girls treating themselves to indulgences such as fancy American hats, flat-out rejecting the old-country styles of their mothers.

Boys sometimes rebelled in darker ways. In the early 1900s, there were more than 1,300 known gangs with more than 25,000 members blanketing the city. The Murderers and the Blackspots were Polish; the Onions, the Torpedoes, and the So Sos were Italian; black gangs included the Wolves and the Twigglies; among the Jewish gangs were the Boundary Gang and the Black Hand Society; the Highbinders were among the Chinese gangs known as tongs. At the top of the pecking order, the Irish "social athletic clubs" were in a class by themselves, wielding a level of power that other gangs could only dream of.

Many of these Irish gangs were tied in with Irish politicians. The boys helped at election time, tearing down the Republican opponents' campaign posters and standing over voters as they cast their ballots at the polls. In return, the sponsoring politicians provided the boys with a clubhouse and athletic equipment. Some clubs were all about sports and roughhousing. The Tri-Street Athletic Club played football, basketball, and baseball. Like all other gangs, they fought with their rivals, but as one member recalled, they were mostly "tomato fights, mud fights, and raids."

Other clubs defended their territory with brutal force. Ragen's Colts was one of the toughest of all. Organized in the first years of the 1900s, the club claimed a territory in the poverty-stricken Irish community of Canaryville, about one square mile in size, bounded on the west by the Union Stock Yard and on the east by the Black Belt. They guarded the deadline with deadly force. The local state's attorney referred to the neighborhood as the training ground for "the Canaryville school of gunmen."

The Colts were both admired and feared. Theirs was the Cadillac of clubhouses, sporting several parlors and a poolroom, a bounty of boxing gloves, baseball team jerseys, bats, and cleats, all paid for by their political patron, Frank Ragen. They were local sports heroes: knockout champions in the boxing ring, victors on the wrestling mat, conquerors on the football field and the baseball diamond, skilled enough to be matched up for an exhibition series of games against the professional Negro League's American Giants in 1917. They were guardians of Irish community life: protectors of the poor and of young Irish girls who might be attacked by predators; defenders of the Catholic Church, throwing rotten food and folding chairs at those who spoke publicly against it. They sponsored social dances, Christmas parties, and Fourth of July picnics for thousands. As one man commented with admiration: "When the Ragens announce an entertainment it means an entertainment, and folks know it."

This powerful gang also acted out a deadly mission to vanquish outsiders. Woe betide another gang or an oblivious youngster from a different neighborhood who happened to set foot in Ragen's territory. Irish, Polish, Italian, Jewish, and most especially blacks—all were fair game. Ragens protected their turf—sometimes with fists, often with a barrage of bricks known as "Irish confetti," sometimes with guns. They issued a warning to anyone who crossed their path: "We intend to run this district. Look out."

The police of Packingtown, like the Colts, were protecting their community. Also like the Colts, the bread and butter

Frank Ragen (left) sitting with the assistant state's attorney Charles Case, and fellow Cook County commissioners John Maloney, Joseph Fitzgerald, and Albert Nowak.

of many Packingtown policemen was dependent on a good word from Frank Ragen or one of his cronies. Ragen made it clear that he thought of the Colts as "a force for good in the stockyards district." The police got the message. Most of the time, when the Colts were at work protecting their turf, the local cops looked the other way.

Gang members, housewives, whiskey swillers, beat cops, politicians, and butchers: each had a role to play, an axe to grind, and a deep loyalty to their own in the community that was Packingtown.

———

Across the deadline, in the decades around the turn of the twentieth century, the Black Belt community was growing. The black population that started as 3,691 people in 1870 stood at 44,103 in 1910, as a steady stream continued to arrive from the South. After a fire in 1874 wiped out the neighborhood where John Jones and many of the earliest black families had settled, most of the growing population had resettled a mile or so south in what came to be called the Black Belt. In the early twentieth century, many whites still lived in this area. But though a few blacks had their homes in various other neighborhoods of the city, by the early 1900s the Black Belt was the center of black community life.

On weekdays, most men and the working women dispersed in the early mornings to places of work that were too far from home to get to on foot. Almost all of the Respectables took the streetcar each day to the wealthy neighborhoods where they cooked and cleaned for the rich, or to the shiny new downtown buildings where they served as cleaning staff or waited tables.

In the early decades of the twentieth century, the streetcar traveled up and down the Black Belt throughout the day, picking up passengers along the way, setting them down again at their destinations. Closest to downtown, it passed through the vice district, home to the Riffraff and the Economically Dispossessed, where painted ladies walked the streets, unemployed men hung out on corners or gathered in bars, and wide-eyed, under-fed children stared out of the cracked windows of dilapidated old buildings or played in the nearby garbage-strewn vacant lots, streets, and alleys.

Traveling south through the Black Belt, the streetcars passed by quiet streets where the Respectables lived in sturdy brick and stone structures mixed with a healthy sprinkling of frame houses and a few apartment buildings. Many of these homes had begun life as single-family dwellings and about half remained such, the others having been divided into doubles or triples. Though better equipped than the homes closer to downtown, many of these residences had few windows, so the rooms were dark and the air was stale. They were furnished with gas lamps instead of electric lights, and multiple families shared toilets located in hallways or even, in some cases, in backyards.

A few avenues to the west, Model T automobiles delivered well-dressed ladies and gentlemen to the doors of imposing three-story brick and stone homes. Here, the small group of the Refined lived with all the luxuries of the day—lush, well-kept lawns and gardens, and a garage leading to ten to twelve gracefully decorated rooms. These mansions had been built by wealthy white families in the late nineteenth century and included two to four bathrooms, electric lighting, gas furnaces, and steam heat.

At last, the streetcar reached the southern edge of the Black Belt, where well-kept lawns and modest gardens adorned streets lined with wooden frame homes, most of which had been divided into two or more comfortably sized apartments. The small businessmen, government workers, and artisans who lived here could not afford the mansions of the Refined, but most of their homes were equipped with indoor plumbing, electric lights, and gas for cooking.

When the school bell rang at dismissal time, the social rooms of Quinn Chapel African Methodist Episcopal and Olivet Baptist churches, Ida Wells-Barnett's Negro Fellowship League, and the Wabash YMCA attracted young people with boys' and girls' clubs, sports teams, and quiet places to read. On weekends, many Respectables gathered in these same spaces for relaxation and social events.

On Sundays, blacks had the choice of more than a dozen churches of various Christian denominations. For many, the church was their rock, spiritually and socially. Many Respectables found comfort and a space to replenish their spirits in the graceful stained-glass-windowed buildings of Olivet Baptist and Quinn Chapel AME. Many of the poorer newly arrived migrants preferred the more down-to-earth experience of smaller, unadorned storefront churches squeezed in among businesses on the commercial strips. At the other end of the spectrum, the Refined tended toward the more formalized ritual, setting up black churches within traditionally white denominations.

For those looking for a good time, the State Street "Stroll," between Twenty-Sixth and Thirty-Ninth Streets, offered a lively place to listen to the jazz greats and exchange the latest gossip. The *Defender* proclaimed it "the popular promenade for the masses and classes." Here on the Stroll, one black man commented, "for a minute or so one forgets the 'Problem.'"

Not for long. The rest of Chicago would not allow it.

EIGHT
A STONE'S THROW

IN THE LATE 1800S, the people of Packingtown and those of the Black Belt ignored one another most of the time. They focused on children to raise, households to run, church, clubs, and local community events. Almost all of them toiled in grinding, low-pay jobs, but usually their paths did not cross. When they did, tensions flared.

Summer was the busy season on the docks along the Chicago River. Starting in 1846, the Chicago harbor was designated by an act of the United States Congress as an official port of entry. Boats arrived from Canada and from points around the United States, bringing in goods of all kinds. Groups of young men—mostly immigrants, a few blacks—roamed the docks, looking for jobs as cooks and sailors on ships, or work as stevedores loading and unloading goods on the docks. All else being equal, immigrants were hired before blacks. But sometimes blacks would win the job with an offer to do the work for lower wages, leaving the immigrants resentful and hostile.

One August day in 1862, an immigrant crew had negotiated themselves a good deal to unload a schooner when a group of blacks

The Chicago Harbor was a busy port in the 1800s.

came along and agreed to do the job for less. The ship captain took the better deal and offered different work to the immigrant men. He failed to recognize that though the immigrants felt injury in losing the job, the insult lay in losing out to blacks. The whites' outrage became painfully clear moments later in a barrage of kicks and punches and a determination to beat the blacks to a pulp that only subsided when police arrived, brandishing their guns.

Two summers later, a dozen or so blacks struck a deal to work on a lumber dock. Immigrants waited it out on the dock until the lumberyard owner showed up, then demanded that he fire the blacks. When he declined to do so, the immigrants gathered together, several hundred in number, and bore down on the black workers, pummeling them right off the dock.

Several days later, another mob gathered to drive blacks away from the docks. The *Tribune* reported, "A man brought the information to Police Headquarters, but [Superintendent of Police] Turtle refused to interfere."

<hr />

When the Civil War ended in 1865, most of Packingtown turned hopes for employment to the newly opened Union Stock Yard. It was clear from the beginning that the giant meatpacking companies were on the same page, filling almost every position with white workers. Sixteen years went by before the Lewis brothers, one a butcher, the other a beef boner, became the first black hires in the Yard. Two decades later, though more than thirty thousand blacks were living in Chicago, only five hundred had jobs in the meatpacking industry.

Those few black souls lucky enough to get work from Swift and the other meatpackers were good union men, treated as members of the butcher brotherhood. One black butcher who died with no family to provide a proper burial was given a full, all-expenses-paid union funeral parade. The union journal reported that seventy-four union men attended the ceremony, which was performed "with the honor and respect that is due to every member" of the union.

In the first few decades after the Union Stock Yard opened, white packinghouse workers were not focused on blacks. They were too busy figuring out how to counter Gustavus Swift and his fellow meatpacking company owners, who were relentlessly creating divisions in order to prevent the workers from showing a united front. The bosses banded together to divide and conquer, and they played their cards well, sometimes raising wages for the butcher aristocracy while coming down hard on the unskilled laborers, then reversing course—always looking to drive a wedge between skilled and unskilled. The bosses maintained the upper hand by staying united, decade after decade. When Gustavus Swift died suddenly in 1903, acknowledged by the *Tribune* as having "revolutionized the industry," his son Louis filled his shoes without missing a beat. In contrast, time after time, quarrels between skilled and unskilled laborers left the work force weak and defeated.

In 1903, the meatpacking laborers got a new leader, a passionate union organizer named Michael Donnelly. Their union, the Amalgamated Meat Cutters and Butcher Workmen of North America, also got a new motto: Unity of all rank and file workers, "from the man who takes the bullock on the hoof until it goes into the hands of the consumer." It was a new day. Interpreters were enlisted to reach out to workers in their own native languages and to translate speeches for them at rallies. For the first time, eastern Europeans were included in decision making.

Women packinghouse employees caused greater commotion among men who did not want to address women's concerns. In the early decades, women workers were easy for the men to ignore. Confined to the canning and labeling departments, they were among the lowest-paid employees. But by the early 1900s, their roles were expanding, and women were tough in defending their rights; they were determined to have a voice in the larger union efforts. This did not sit well with some men, who worried about women infringing on "man's work." But the majority thought it was best to include them—skilled and unskilled, men and women together.

Donnelly worked to inspire passion for the union, and when he felt the laborers' union spirit was strong enough, he called a strike. Midday on July 12, 1904, twenty-eight thousand men and women employed by meatpacking companies throughout the Stock Yard put away their tools and walked off the job. The strike was to be orderly and peaceful: signs posted in five languages reminded strikers to "Obey the union's rules to molest no person or property, and abide strictly by the laws of the country." Street fighting began nine hours later.

Michael Donnelly organized the packinghouse workers and led the 1904 strike.

Under cover of darkness, a wagon driver approached the Yard, hauling a load of mattresses for delivery to Swift & Company. With his workers on strike, Swift was preparing to bring in outsiders to take their place and to provide the strikebreakers with temporary sleeping quarters inside the Stock Yard. This tactic was commonly used by industrialists to combat strikes and was well-known among laborers.

Out of the silence, nearby saloons sprang to life, disgorging hundreds of strikers who blocked the roadway, overturning the cart and dragging the driver away. A couple of hours later, fifty men recruited from the streets of the Black Belt were spirited into the Stock Yard, where they looked to get a good night's sleep, with or without mattresses, before taking the place of strikers on the early-morning shift.

The next day, the Yard was quietly active. Strikers stopped in to pick up their last paychecks. Foremen and superintendents, along with a few laborers who decided to stay on the job and the recruited blacks, were doing what they could to keep the disassembly line running. As the day went on, their numbers were increased by more job seekers looking to take advantage of the opportunity to replace strikers. According to the *Tribune,* men and women, Greeks, Italians, Poles, and Scandinavians signed up to fill in.

A crowd that included many children during the 1904 Union Stock Yard strike.
The rocks on the ground might have been used later against the strikebreakers.

Strikers idled in bars around the Yard, staring out the window at the steady stream of men and women the packers were bringing in. It started with local residents. A few days later, trainloads of out-of-towners were being deposited at the Great Gate of the Union Stock Yard. Many had the familiar look of newly arrived immigrants. Most visible, and most upsetting to the strikers, were the groups of blacks up from the South.

The stories of the black strikebreakers died with the men who lived them, never recorded for future generations. But their decision to answer the packers' call might have been based on thinking like Horace Cayton's. As a young black man during World War I, Cayton made the acquaintance of a white union member. His new friend "Red" lectured him: "I got nothing against the colored. . . . But on the whole the colored don't make good union men. The white bosses have held them down so long they can't believe in anything except the rich. . . . The bosses make scabs out of Negroes to divide the workers. Negroes shouldn't let themselves be used but they do." To this, Cayton had an honest reply: "We can't trust any white man. It's the same with every last one of you. We colored have to wait and be patient. . . . What it all comes down to is that we're not equals. Hell, I don't trust you. We're supposed to get our pie in the sky when we die?" Cayton was clear: "I'd break a strike to get a decent job."

As trainload after trainload of black strikebreakers from the South rolled into the Stock Yard, they were met with violent anger. At regular intervals along the way, white strikers and their families stood along the train route and heaved barrages of stones and bricks. The strikers were consumed with hatred—not limited to strikebreakers but directed at blacks as a race.

Strikebreakers were safe inside the Yard, but those who journeyed beyond the Great Gate at day's end walked into danger. Mobs of strikers massed for attack, usually launching a hail of stones followed by a melee of fists and kicks.

White strikebreakers were sometimes attacked, but blacks were the focus of the most vicious fury. Three black strikebreakers watching a baseball game in a vacant lot caught the attention of a Packingtown mob and were quickly engulfed in a swirl of raging humanity. One of the blacks pulled out a gun in self-defense and shot an attacker in the cheek. When police arrived, they dispersed the mob and arrested the black man. Another black man was beginning a streetcar ride home with his ten-year-old son when the pair caught the eye of some strikers. As the streetcar made its way along the avenue, the group of strikers chasing the car and throwing stones snowballed to a mob of nearly two hundred. When the streetcar stopped, the father and his son made a run for it, all the while bombarded by stones. Both were badly injured.

Packingtown rallied around the strikers. Wives took up work outside the home, earning what they could to sustain their families over the rough patch. Sons and daughters joined their mothers to support their fathers as they marched or picketed around the Yard. The local saloons and other businesses formed a Stockyards Aid Society, and relief stations distributed groceries to those families nearing starvation. Small business owners refused to cash checks of individuals who were crossing the picket line. Parish leaders used the pulpit to lend "the arm of the Church to what we believe is a righteous cause." Local politicians chimed in. The Irish Justice of the Stockyards District Police Court, with jurisdiction over minor crimes in that neighborhood, dismissed more than eighty percent of claims brought against strikers accused of violent attacks. This blatant disregard of the law outraged the packinghouse owners; future cases were removed to the court of another community where the law was better upheld. Along with the community institutions, individuals donated what they could. A bride who received money pinned to her wedding dress in the Polish tradition was reported to have

Police escorted strikebreakers to the packinghouses during the strike.

regifted it to the strikers' relief fund. Stories like this were every-where.

Still, as the strike wore on, food and money were running out. Some days more than six hundred families stood in line for a handout of rice, oatmeal, potatoes, flour, and coffee, along with a little meat if there was any to be had. Some days, shelves at the commissary were bare long before day's end, leaving hundreds to walk away with nothing. One woman wept as she cradled her nine-month-old infant, having just been told there was no milk to give her. Another family with eight children was reduced to living on crusts of bread for nearly a week.

Packinghouse owners provided a male escort for women strikebreakers.

As Labor Day rolled around, the strikers' prospects looked dim. In the end, though the rank and file wanted to keep on fighting, union leader Donnelly knew they could not win. On September 8, he called off the strike. The immigrants had lost.

~~~

As the summer of 1904 faded away, disillusionment sat heavy over Packingtown and the Black Belt. Powerful currents of distrust collided as immigrants and blacks sold each other out and business owners did their best to capitalize on the divisions.

The packers had won the latest round. But Louis Swift and his fellow industrialists could not rest easy; a new standoff was always just around the corner, requiring new strategies to keep the bosses one step ahead of their workers.

The immigrants of Packingtown had come together to demand a better life, to no avail. Mary McDowell, a leading settlement house social worker, observed that the defeated strikers seemed "unmanly and without self-respect." They finally had stood together—skilled and unskilled—with nothing to show for it. A national union leader, Homer Call, questioned the immigrants' access to the American dream: "Shall the standard of the most poorly paid workers of Europe be established by the packers as the standard of life for American citizens?"

The strikers' confidence in the union was destroyed. Over the coming months, they deserted in droves. They resented Swift and the other big bosses who had mercilessly beaten them down. But perhaps more than anything else, they blamed blacks for their predicament. In their eyes, black people were, and always would be, the "scab" race.

When the packinghouse strike ended, the pre-strike configurations settled back into place. Even in defeat, the immigrants regained their dominance over laboring positions in the Stock Yard, and black strikebreakers returned to the South. Before long, however, blacks would be back. This time, it would be to stay.

PART THREE

UP FROM THE SOUTH

I pick up my life
And take it with me
And I put it down in Chicago

—Langston Hughes
"One-Way Ticket"

*Overleaf: The Union
Stock Yards.*

NINE
A HIGHER CALL

IN 1917, IMMIGRANTS AND BLACKS ALIKE, along with men of every ilk across the United States, left their Chicago homes, their families, and their jobs, and took up President Woodrow Wilson's call to enter the Great War that was raging in Europe: to "fight for the things which we have always carried nearest our hearts—for democracy . . . and [to] make the world itself at last free."

European Americans responded with patriotism for their adopted land. But the President's words resonated with a special significance for America's blacks. In Chicago, they volunteered for duty in large numbers, a fact the *Chicago Defender* proudly pointed out: "Let us take notice of the loyalty of Colored American citizens by way of contrast, with but a half chance to live, how they are accepting the whole chance to die." Another newspaper commented, "Many indulge the hope that America's entry in the conflict to 'make the world safe for democracy,' will result in giving a new meaning to democracy in America." This was a convergence of interests that blacks had been looking for.

In October, Chicago's all-black Eighth Infantry Regiment prepared to leave on the long journey across the Atlantic Ocean to the

factories for food, clothes, and munitions for soldiers fighting in Europe, and the factories were looking for new workers. In February 1917, the *Defender* counseled, "For the hardworking man there is plenty of work [in the North]—if you really want it. The *Defender* says come."

The **Chicago Defender** *spreads word of the Great Migration, August 19, 1916. A black man is shown waking up from sleep on a bale of cotton, symbolizing his independence from the southern economy.*

The Illinois Central Railroad runs a thousand miles south to north down the middle of the United States. Its southernmost point is the city of New Orleans. Its northern terminus is the city of Chicago. In between, it chugs through the lush rolling hills of Mississippi, through mile after mile of cotton fields and pine forests, past towns and small cities dotting the landscape. In the years 1916 to 1918, thousands of southern blacks boarded the train and traveled north to a new life. In 1917, Charles S. Johnson, a black sociologist and later the first black president of Fisk University, captured some of their stories in interviews with Mississippi migrants about their move to Chicago.

Mr. Henderson (first name unknown) was a railroad man hailing from those southern Mississippi hills. He had worked the railroads for fifteen years, making enough money to build his wife a house on a nice property of a hundred acres of land. His take-home pay was good—one hundred and twenty-five dollars each month. He felt satisfied with his accomplishments. But the train took him to places far away from his small slice of happiness, and the world he saw was full of pain and sorrow. The stories he could tell! On a stop through Mobile, Alabama, a black man accosted him, crying and begging for a ride up north. It seemed his business had been snatched right out from under him, taken over by a white man, and there was nothing he could do. Neither man nor law would come to his aid in Mobile. He was left with no way to earn a living. The man's plight touched Mr. Henderson's heart.

Other stories, closer to home, weighed heavily on Mr. Henderson's mind. Sometime around 1913, a black man had killed a white policeman just a few miles from Henderson's home. An enraged mob killed the black man, then continued in its fury to destroy property owned by blacks in the surrounding area. A couple of years later, a trainman's beautiful mixed-race wife, alone at night while her husband was away on a run, was visited by a white man who thought he might just have "a good time" with her. Trips away were never the same again for Henderson, always tinged with anxiety about leaving his wife alone. He daydreamed of moving up north. He had been there from time to time on railroad passes; he liked what he saw. But he also knew there were no jobs open to him that could pay like his current one or offer the same security. So Henderson decided to bide his time.

As 1916 rolled around, excitement was building along Henderson's route through Mississippi. In Meridian, a Mrs. Hunter (first name unknown) returned from a trip to the big city of Birmingham, Alabama, brimming with news. She'd heard that many people were leaving Birmingham for the North, for the higher wages they said they could earn in northern cities. Mrs. Hunter found the information hard to believe. Wages in Birmingham were already twice as high as in Meridian. She could not imagine an even better job market up north, but she urged her son to go to Chicago and see with his own eyes. Three weeks later he wrote, "Everything is just like they say, if not better." He made arrangements to bring his family to join him—first his wife to set up house; later, when all was ready, Mrs. Hunter would bring their six children.

A little down the way, in Hattiesburg, the *Defender* was generating excited conversation at Robert Horton's barbershop. Proud of his shop's status as the community hub, Horton took forty to fifty copies of the *Defender* every week, magnanimously distributing them to customers at cost. The *Defender*'s talk of political freedom in the North fascinated him. Blacks didn't just have the right to vote; they had the right to vote their own into office.

Horton could think of no greater satisfaction. But he was cautious. His barbershop, his Hattiesburg clientele, was his livelihood. It seemed too risky to go up north and start from scratch. He had been tempted once, when he traveled to New Orleans to attend his daughter's graduation from Straight University. Looking to pass

Moving day in the Black Belt.

some time while his daughter was otherwise engaged, he had sauntered down to the local barbershop, where he met a man who was talking up the North, promising a bushelful of jobs, offering free train tickets to Chicago. Horton shook his head. He wasn't ready. But he couldn't dismiss the idea, and he mulled it over with family and friends when he returned home to Hattiesburg.

The word was spreading. Someone up north had sent a letter to someone in Georgia, and that letter was carefully handed from person to person, winding its way across state lines to Laurel, Mississippi, where it was taken up and read out loud at a meeting of the Sisters Home Mission.

Back in nearby Hattiesburg, a family—the Martins (first names unknown)—decided to test the waters. Mr. Martin went up first and reported back that wages in Chicago were high and that for the first time in his life, he felt like a man. Sell everything and join me, he told his wife. Mrs. Martin showed the letter to her friends, who were excited, and to her pastor, who was very much against it. But she paid him no mind. She sold her house, chickens, cow, and as much furniture as she could, and led a group of ten to Chicago.

All these people would need lodging: a friend of Horton's owned a boarding house in Hattiesburg, and that's what she concluded. She sold her Hattiesburg place and opened a new boarding house up north, telling her Hattiesburg boarders that she would give them "privileges" at her place in Chicago. And Mr. Horton passed along names and addresses of people he knew who would be needing a place to stay when they reached their destination.

The stories piled up. One girl who had been making two dollars per week in Meridian wrote home to say she was now working in the Chicago stockyards and making two dollars per day.

Northern schools were better, too. In the South, many black children were allowed to attend school only a few months each year; from planting time to harvest, they worked long days on the farm. Even when school was in session, getting an education was not easy. The school system separated blacks and whites in unequal schools. Many black children had to walk miles each day to get to a one-room shack supplied with just a few used books. Most did not attend high school at all. They lived too far away to attend any of the few high schools open to black students. Black teachers, though highly respected in their community, were paid very little. The stories from up north painted a much rosier picture of education in Chicago. Bosses did not pull children out of school, and there were schools within walking distance for everyone; the school year was six whole months long, and teachers got monthly pay of thirty dollars.

The buzz grew and grew. People were leaving the South and heading to Chicago in parties of twenty, sixty, even more.

This migrant family has just arrived in Chicago with suitcases and overcoats.

Some southern whites did not take this well. As a national black leader, Booker T. Washington, put it, the southern way of life was dependent on "the Negro and the mule." Whites tried to entice "their" blacks to stay, talking up the perils of the North— race riots and cold weather, both of which would bring misery and death. It was better, they counseled, to stay put with friends and family and the familiar life of the sunny South. But blacks didn't appear to be listening. And that troublemaking *Defender* seemed to be everywhere the whites turned. The thing to do was to keep that rabble-rousing nonsense out of black hands. In Meridian, Mississippi, where Mrs. Hunter lived, the chief of police confiscated the *Defender* from men selling it on the street.

For the most part, blacks did not protest. In the South, whites could take out their anger in any way they wanted. To blacks' way of thinking, there was no sense in suffering the humiliation of public tongue-lashings and insults. And it wasn't worth the risk that some white man would respond by beating them to a pulp or dragging them off to jail or even taking them out in the night and hanging them from a tree. But they quietly placed mail orders to receive the paper in the privacy of their own homes.

Mrs. Hunter, who had brought news of the North from Birmingham to Meridian, looked around. All her Mississippi friends were leaving, and country people—not her sort—were moving in. Life was becoming quite dull. She sold what she could, disappointed that she could get only seven hundred dollars for a house that was worth twice as much. She wrapped up the family's affairs, readied the children, and boarded the Illinois Central, resigned to whatever Chicago might bring.

Horton's Hattiesburg barbershop and community hub, too, was getting quieter and quieter. The city was clearing out. News of departures became a part of everyday conversation. From those who had "the northern fever," a standard goodbye was making the rounds: "Only the waters of Lake Michigan can cure me."

The whites' dire warnings were failing. Those looking to keep their black help from leaving resorted to setting booby traps to stop them. The Hattiesburg police had a plan: they would block every entrance to the train depot, making it impossible for blacks to purchase tickets; then they would arrest anyone trying to board without a ticket. They felt triumphant as a train pulled in, took on white passengers, and then chugged out of the station with no blacks aboard. But the blacks would not be denied and swung themselves onto the train at the very last second as it pulled out of town.

Sometimes justice did not prevail. Railroad man Mr. Henderson knew this. A friend of his had gone north and sent back a half-

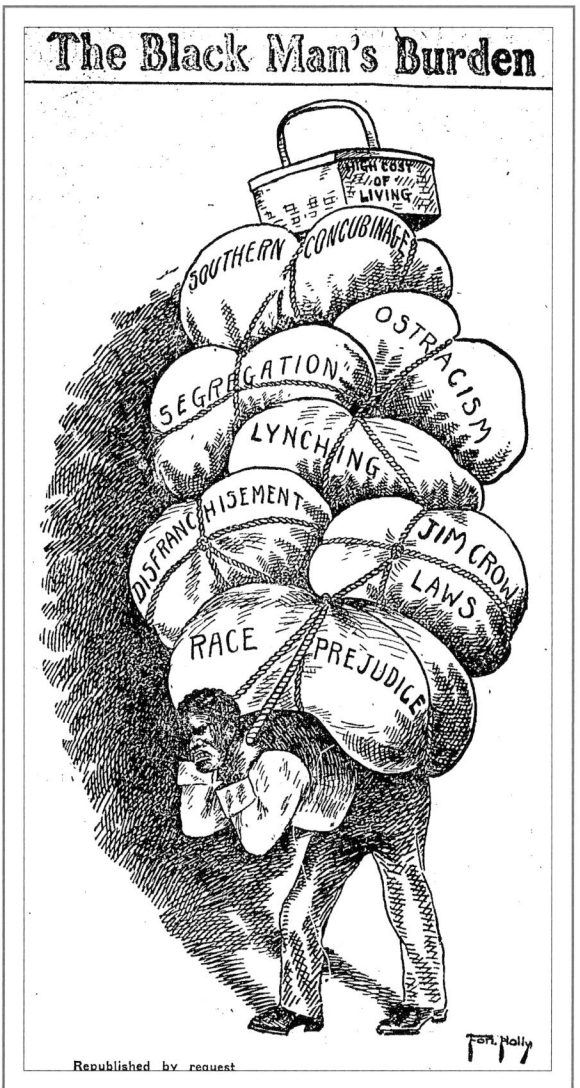

This editorial cartoon in the Chicago Defender (January 6, 1917) illustrates the many obstacles facing blacks at the time of the Great Migration.

fare ticket for his wife to join him, but when she got to the station, the station agent refused to accept the ticket, and there was nothing she could do about it.

Henderson thought about his own life. Fifteen years he had put into the railroad, and he had no seniority, no rights or benefits, to show for it because of his race. He thought about the black folks his train carried up north, leaving everything they knew for an uncertain future. And they were making it; there were jobs for the taking. He decided it was time to act. He asked for his seniority. Just as he had always feared, he was fired on the spot. But he was moving on. When his superintendent reversed the decision and offered Henderson his job back, he turned it down. He was on his way to Chicago.

The barber Robert Horton was a deacon in his church. Cautious by nature, he watched his people leave, in a trickle at first, then in a massive wave. He was convinced that this was not about one person or one family or even about one town. This was about a people, and, as Horton saw it, they were guided by the hand of God. The time he had been praying for had come. In 1917, he packed his things and headed for Chicago.

ELEVEN

A REAL PLACE FOR NEGROES

THE ILLINOIS CENTRAL carried its passengers through the green hills and forests of Mississippi, up through Tennessee and Kentucky, across the bridge over the Ohio River into Cairo, Illinois, over the flat prairie land of central Illinois. As the train drew close to Chicago, greenery and blue sky were replaced by a canopy of gray smoke spewed into the air by the nearby steel mills, and passengers could begin to anticipate the gritty might of the city. When the train pulled into Chicago's Illinois Central station, passengers were disgorged into the hustle and bustle of a city that was exciting but also immensely intimidating. Ida Wells-Barnett observed, "They arrived in Chicago in every conceivable state of unpreparedness."

The station's grand three-story marble waiting room was housed below a forty-five-foot vaulted ceiling, shimmering under immense shafts of light that poured through long windows lining the room. There, hundreds of people were rushing about.

Many in the Hattiesburg contingent had written back and forth about the specifics of their arrival. The luckiest migrants were scooped up out of the chaos by waiting friends or relatives. Others arrived with only an address in hand, expected to find their way to prearranged housing. Some came with no one expecting them, making the journey on faith that it would all work out somehow, arriving unannounced and unequipped, with no planned course of action beyond their first steps off the train. One migrant recalled his fear of being "completely lost . . . afraid to ask anyone where to go."

But the city was prepared for them. In that year of 1917, the Chicago Urban League, a branch of the National Urban League headquartered in New York City, had been founded with the specific mission of integrating black migrants into city life—helping them with jobs, housing, and social adjustment.

It all began at the train station. Experienced black Urban League staff worked side by side with white women workers from the Travelers Aid Society to get migrants' first steps on the right path. As new arrivals with bewildered faces entered the waiting room, they were met by offers of assistance. Those with addresses in hand were told how to get where they wanted to go; those with no contacts were directed to available temporary rooms in boarding houses, such as the one run by Robert Horton's friend, or sent to board as lodgers with families who were looking to take in a little extra money. Communication was difficult at times. Many migrant men had learned in the South to be wary of speaking to white women. For their part, many frustrated aides had difficulty trying to understand the migrants' southern drawl. A business card was pressed into the palm of each newcomer, encouraging a visit to the Urban League. Then migrants were sent out into their newly adopted city, walking or riding the streetcar toward the address that was, as of this moment, home.

If You are a Stranger in the City

If you want a job   If you want a place to live
If you are having trouble with your employer
If you want information or advice of any kind

CALL UPON

The CHICAGO LEAGUE ON URBAN CONDITIONS AMONG NEGROES

3719 South State Street

Telephone Douglas 9098   T. ARNOLD HILL, Executive Secretary

No charges—no fees. We want to help YOU

SELF-HELP

1. Do not loaf. Get a job at once.
2. Do not live in crowded rooms. Others can be obtained.
3. Do not carry on loud conversations in street cars and public places.
4. Do not keep your children out of school.
5. Do not send for your family until you get a job.
6. Do not think you can hold your job unless you are industrious, sober, efficient and prompt.

   Cleanliness and fresh air are necessary for good health. In case of sickness send immediately for a good physician. Become an active member in some church as soon as you reach the city.

Issued by

Aldis F 6

Card distributed by the Chicago Urban League.

For those who hopped the streetcar, the first instinct was to move to the back. But here were blacks sitting next to whites. One migrant recalled, "I just held my breath, for I thought any minute [the whites] would start something." Some whites did object to blacks taking seats "all over the car," but it was rare for anyone to cause a fuss. Some migrants found this unsettling and preferred the comfort of the familiar seats in the rear. Others were exhilarated. One migrant remembered thinking, "This is a real place for Negroes."

The streetcar rolled through the Black Belt, allowing passengers a good look at the community. The poet Langston Hughes recalled arriving in 1918: "South State Street was in its glory then, a teeming Negro street with crowded theaters, restaurants, and cabarets. And excitement from noon to noon. Midnight was like day. The street was full of workers and gamblers, prostitutes and pimps, church folks and sinners."

T. Arnold Hill was tasked with leading the new Chicago branch of the National Urban League. He planted the offices in the midst of this black metropolis, rolled up his sleeves, and went to work. His goal was to empower the wave of migrants rolling into town to become productive citizens of their adopted city. A few blocks away, A. L. Jackson, executive director of the local Wabash Street YMCA, was pushing in the same direction. Other groups, such as Ida Wells-Barnett's Negro Fellowship League, were pursuing the same goal.

The Urban League focused on connecting the migrants with jobs and housing, the YMCA on teaching them the ways and expectations of people in the North. Their work was respected in the black community. Many who could ill afford it gave a dollar here, a dollar there, to show their support.

Hill and Jackson were the most powerful black team around. They knew that to get anywhere, they needed to work with the powerhouses in the city who held the keys to jobs, housing, and

Mother and child in the Black Belt, 1919.

social services. And so they went a-courting, reaching out to members of the black Refined and also to white business leaders.

Louis Swift and other owners of the large industries in dire need of workers gladly joined forces with Hill and Jackson. Who better to teach the southern blacks how to be good workers than men of their own race? And something else made it worth throwing in money and programmatic support. Swift and his fellow chiefs of commerce were banking on the likelihood that Hill and Jackson would have the sense not to bite the hand that fed them.

TWELVE

A JOB, ANY JOB

MOST BLACKS LOOKING TO LEAVE the South were encouraged by the possibility of a better life up north. Hundreds of southerners sent letters to the *Defender* and to the Urban League inquiring about a job, any job. A woman from Alabama carefully set out her qualifications for work as a washerwoman: "For seven previous years I bore the reputation of a first class laundress in Selma. I have much experience with all of the machines in this laundry." She asked for "clear information how to get a good position." A Florida longshoreman made it plain that he was willing to take whatever was offered: "I used to have from 150 to 200 men under my charge. They thought I was capable in doing the work and at the meantime I am willing to do anything."

Former farmers, stonemasons, and plasterers became general laborers; a barber became a house painter; a blacksmith set up shop as a barber; a teacher took work in the Union Stock Yard; a pastor became a fireman. For many, the Urban League business card they were given at the railroad station was all they had to go on. They were eager to see exactly what this Urban League could do for them.

From the very start, the migrants liked what they saw at the Urban League offices. Pride surged in their chests as they were ushered in and seated before the desks of well-dressed black men and women who asked them questions about their experience and provided leads on jobs. On the other side of the desk, League staff sized up the migrants, trying, as an Urban League report explained, "to fit the workers to the jobs and the jobs to the workers." There was much to teach in a short time to these newly arrived migrants, who had never before seen anything like the parade of cows on Swift's disassembly line. Gone was the slow, irregular way of southern farm life; Swift and the other northern bosses demanded speed and reliability. As one staffer saw it, the Urban League's job was to develop "in the worker's mind her personal responsibility to become a regular and efficient employee."

From the League offices, migrants were sent out to job sites: some to steel mills, tanneries, or railcar shops; most to the stockyards, where the need was greatest and the commute was shortest

Dozens of men waited in line outside the Chicago Urban League office.

from homes in the Black Belt. The number of blacks employed in the Yard increased quickly, from around a thousand in 1915 to more than ten thousand in 1918.

Those hired were shown to their new jobs, the jobs no one else had wanted, the hardest, dirtiest, least tolerable work left at the bottom of the barrel after the white men and then the white women had taken their pick. The newly arrived could not help but notice the unfair pecking order. They particularly resented that they, who were native to American soil, were passed over by their supervisors in favor of recently arrived immigrants. One man complained that his boss passed him over when giving out overtime hours, favoring Polish workers who had less seniority. Another remarked that complaining about unfair treatment was risky because his boss would try to "burn" him out with work.

Most southerners chose not to dwell on the favoritism they saw. Eyes were turned toward making good in the northern way that offered so much more possibility than the South. One foundry worker laid out his goals: "I'm an expert now . . . I can quit any time I want to, but the longer I work the more money it is for me. . . . I am planning to educate my girl with the best of them, buy a home before I'm too old, and make life comfortable for my family." Down south, explained one man, you "had to take whatever they paid you." In Chicago, there was cash in your pocket and a steady stream of new job openings if the current one wasn't working out. One woman expressed the pleasure of not having "an overseer always standing over you." It felt like freedom.

Louis Swift and the other industrialists liked what they saw: T. Arnold Hill and his staff were cutting waste and adding to profits by weeding out the bad apples and sending along the good ones; A. L. Jackson and his YMCA staff were creating a positive worker mindset, teaching worker efficiency, and handing out good advice on how to handle racial tension on the job.

Hill and Jackson understood their value and played it to the hilt. Hill jumped on every chance to bend the ear of the industrialists, explaining why promotion of blacks to foremen would reduce conflict and increase efficiency. The Urban League shaped the attitude of bosses with lectures on topics such as "How to Handle Negro Labor." Jackson won programs to educate newly arrived workers, selling the idea as a good way for business owners to win black allegiance. In this way, workers learned valuable skills, signing up for company-sponsored "Efficiency Clubs" that provided training on topics such as "Progress of the Negro in the Packing Industry" and "Electricity and Its Use in the Yards."

Jackson further parlayed the desire of the packers and other manufacturing business owners to win the hearts and minds of

Captioned "A Negro Amateur Baseball Team," this photo shows the Swift Premiums.

their black employees, setting up a host of company-sponsored social groups. Thousands of fans spent lazy summer evenings rooting for their family and friends on teams in an industrial baseball league that included the Swift Premiums. Others proudly gave formal concerts in company-sponsored singing groups. One meatpacking business owner handed out free YMCA memberships to black workers after one year of employment. Migrants responded with enthusiasm. One of them recalled, "The packing houses in Chicago for a while seemed to be everything." Another man summed up his experience in Chicago more broadly: the "place [is] just full of life."

THIRTEEN
FULL TO BURSTING

THE BLACK BELT WAS, IN FACT, full to bursting. This was not a good thing. The problem was a mathematical one. In the six years from 1914 to 1920, the black population doubled, with most of that growth coming in 1916 to 1918, but the number of homes open to black Chicagoans stayed the same. Some whites living in the area moved away, but most stayed put. There simply was not enough room in the Black Belt for everyone.

Mr. Horton's rooming-house owner friend from Hattiesburg did her best to give new folks temporary shelter. Her seven rooms were always crammed to the gills, with as many as twenty-one men boarding at a time and five to six new referrals every day. In one three-month period, for example, she temporarily housed 698 people. Families with extra space in rundown but roomy dwellings helped out too, taking in lodgers to make a little extra money. Still, there were not enough rooms to accommodate the waves of migrants that continued to flood in. The sight of newcomers wandering the streets at all hours was part of the cityscape.

Some, like the Hattiesburg clan, were organized, finding a concentration of homes where they could settle down together and recreate their community from down south. But this happy fate was not the norm. In the summer of 1917, an Urban League survey of realtors took a single-day snapshot that tallied 664 applicants for housing but only fifty homes available to them.

The overpopulation created a breeding ground for illness. Six out of every seven people struck down by tuberculosis in Chicago were black. Their prospects of escape to a healthier environment were dim. With so little housing for so many people, landlords could charge whatever came into their heads. As one man commented, "Rent goes up whenever people think of it." Most blacks did not have the resources to get away to more sanitary conditions.

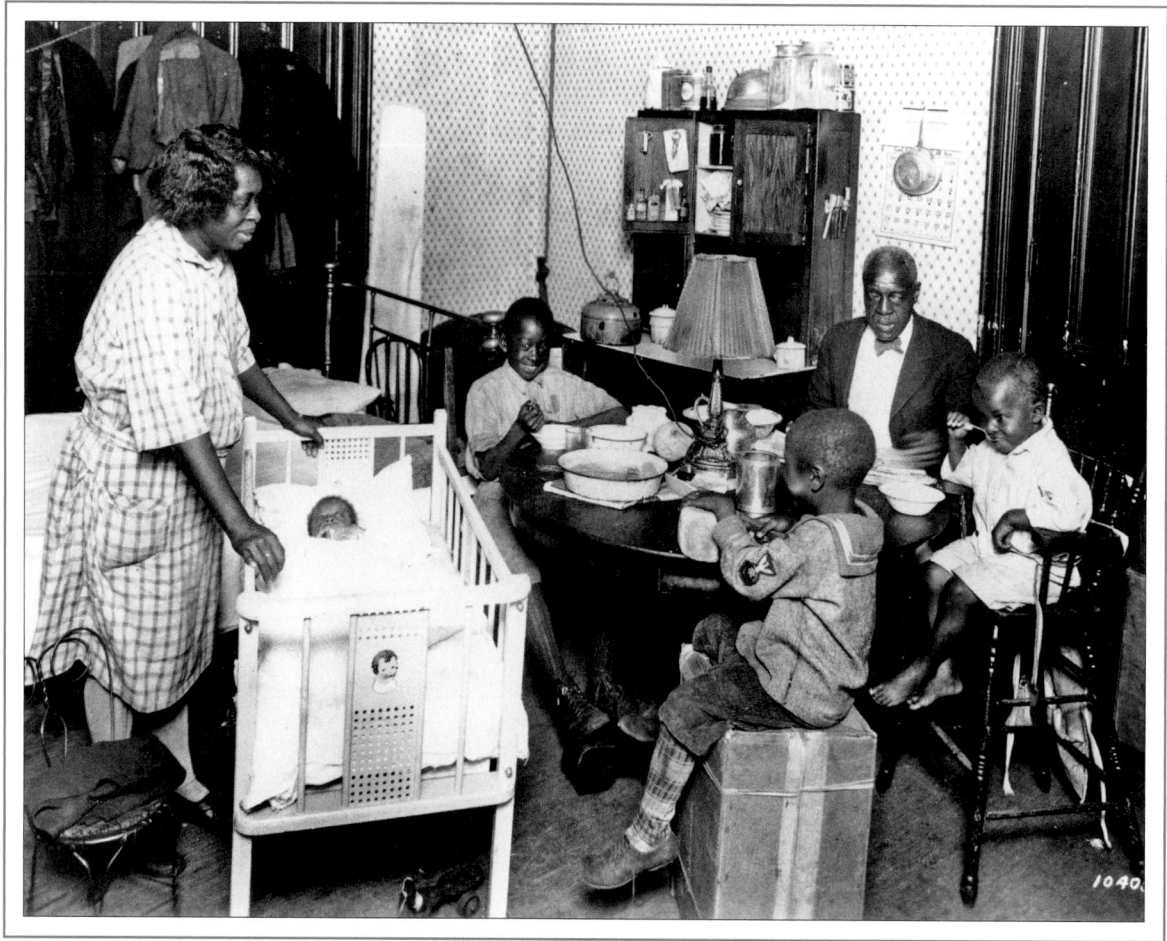

This black family lived in a one-room apartment.

The biggest surprise lay in store for the migrants who had sold property and brought cash from the South, expecting to purchase a nice home in their new city. Upon arrival, one look was all they needed to see that the Black Belt was not set up to offer them what they were looking for. A quick investigation of other neighborhoods around the city turned up all sorts of apartments and houses for rent or sale. But upon inquiry, blacks found themselves politely or not-so-politely turned away.

The middle-class whites living to the east formed property owners' protective associations to hold the line against a black "invasion." They made their purpose painfully clear to blacks. One real estate dealer bluntly stated: "You people are not admitted to our society." To the west, Ragen's Colts and other gangs held the line in Packingtown in a different way, using the tried-and-true threat of violence: "There's a nigger! Let's get him!"

Blacks tried to make a go of it within the boundaries laid out for them. The owner of a black baseball team remembered that he "moved four times . . . seeking desirable living quarters." But as the days turned into weeks, into months, into years, the day-in, day-out smells, sights, and sounds that accompany extreme congestion crowded the minds of the people, leaving room for little else. And a few fed-up souls began to push back against efforts of whites in nearby neighborhoods to lock them out.

A black choral society.

Dixie," referred to in a letter to the editor as "the more unfortunate and ignorant race," and discussed in many articles as "the Negro Problem."

Children, now attending the schools that their parents had been so excited about, were learning that many of their white teachers did not think they were capable of being educated. Most migrant children found their first steps into school directed down the hall to the "subnormal" classroom for "retarded" students. Some teachers recognized that the lack of schooling in the South left these children behind and found that many caught up quickly. But one commented that the children had "no sticking qualities" and another opined that blacks quickly reached "the limit of [their] mental ability."

Though many schools in the Black Belt had mostly black children in their attendance zone, all schools included some whites. On the school playground, the youngest children delighted in interracial games of tag or hopscotch or jump rope. Even so, prejudice sometimes reared its ugly head. One school choir's excitement about performing for immigrant children in Packingtown evaporated when the singers were pelted with stones by some neighborhood toughs.

At the high school down the street, their older brothers and sisters no longer socialized together. They gathered in the school lunchroom at separate black and white lunch tables, and after school, those black students who were not on athletic teams made their way to Ida Wells-Barnett's Negro Fellowship League or the Wabash YMCA, a church club, or a neighborhood park, or hung out on the street. White students were invited to stay and participate in all-white after-school social clubs.

Whether coming from work, home, or school, or just out for a good time on the town, there was a decent chance for blacks to cross paths with trouble. Immigrant gangs were often on the prowl, looking for victims to jump. The Barnetts' sons found themselves under regular attack by white boys in their own neighborhood. Ida kept a pistol in the house.

Calling the police was not necessarily the right decision in these situations. One black man on his way home from work learned the hard way. As he stood on the elevated train platform near Packingtown, a mob jumped him, pounding his body with punches. The policeman stopping to break it up seized the black man, hauled him off to the police station, and threw him in jail for the next five days. The mob was left to search out its next victim.

Just catching a policeman's attention might well cause a black person's heart to skip a beat. A typical example was a raid on a bar following a vague tip that someone was gambling. Police rushed in, arrested everyone in sight with no evidence of wrongdoing by anyone, threw them all in a holding cell for the night, and hauled them off for fingerprinting the next day.

There was no public outrage at this kind of tactics. The *Tribune* bought in to the stereotypes, often reporting allegations against blacks without any evidence of their truth and skipping a retraction when innocence came to light. One principal said out loud what many were thinking, expressing concern over "the emotional tendency of the colored to knife and kill."

In the face of this systemic disrespect, blacks were encouraged by their leaders to hold their heads high. The primary message

Blacks at a police station being searched for weapons.

they received was that the migrants were no longer in the land of white supremacy. The *Defender* counseled, "Quit calling the foreman 'boss.' Leave that word dropped in the Ohio River. . . . We call people up here, Mister This or Mister That." As to white co-workers, "Treat them as you want them to treat you—AS A MAN." One school principal observed that black mothers instructed their children "not to take anything from a white child." And they encouraged their teens to stay in school, even in the face of prejudice. Life was not easy. But it was a new day, and a new black consciousness was taking hold.

Black leaders backed their talk with political muscle. Robert Horton had marveled, even before the migration, at the power of blacks living in Chicago to elect their own. The first black alderman had been elected in 1915, and he was later elected to Congress. The previous black congressman had served thirty years before.

Also in 1915, blacks played a decisive role in electing the mayor, Republican William Thompson. "Big Bill," a white man, was a larger-than-life hero to the black community. One black leader, Reverend Archibald Carey, went so far as to put Thompson on a pedestal with Abraham Lincoln. Big Bill, whom the *Defender* called "the spectacular, nervy Mayor of Chicago," publicly spoke out against the slights that blacks found so demeaning, and made a great show of celebrating their successes. He banned screenings of the racist film *The Birth of a Nation* and trumpeted black heroes like the boxer Jack Johnson. In 1915, Black Belt voters were crucial to Big Bill's victory. Returning the favor, Big Bill appointed black leaders to high-profile positions in government.

Buoyed by this example of success, thousands of new migrants massing in the city's second ward in 1917 and 1918 took to the polls and elected two black aldermen to represent them. The Black Belt shone as a symbol of the power of the ballot all across black America.

"Thompson for Mayor" poster.

By 1918, nearly fifty thousand black migrants were settled into their new city. They took up work in the stockyards, steel mills, and other industrial plants, accomplishing what they had been recruited to do. But they also exercised a new freedom to make decisions of their own—about work, housing, school, voting. And as the people of Chicago were learning, these newly arrived black citizens were making decisions that could affect them all.

PART FOUR
REAPING THE WHIRLWIND

Like men we'll face the murderous, cowardly pack,
Pressed to the wall, dying, but fighting back!

—Claude McKay
"If We Must Die"

FIFTEEN
TENSIONS RISING

In 1917, a newly organized meatpacking workers' union called the Stockyards Labor Council made plans to bring the new black laborers into the fold. The worker shortage caused by the war left the shapeup empty and laborers in high demand. Union leaders John Fitzpatrick and William Z. Foster were galvanized by the golden opportunity for a big union win if they could just bring all the workers together before the bosses divided them. To drum up excitement, Fitzpatrick and Foster tapped talented men to lead— one to solidify support among Johnny Joyce's cattle butchers, another to organize blacks. John Kikulski, a rousing speaker much beloved in the Polish community, was tasked with energizing the eastern Europeans.

Louis Swift's goal was to keep black and white workers separated. The packers kept track of Fitzpatrick and Foster's efforts, and they did not like what they saw. If the union could bring all workers together, it would be a powerful force to contend with. Louis Swift recalled his father's strategy: "When . . . the strikes threatened his prosperity through no fault of his own, then he proceeded to do everything he could to break them." The packers needed to head off trouble by stirring up conflicts among the workers to weaken the union. As an initial step, they were pleased to find an ally in a black small-time newspaper editor and entrepreneur, Richard E. Parker.

Parker did not trust unions. He was in good company there. More than a few blacks could still feel the sting of the waiters' union double-cross. Others could tell a story or two about vicious name-calling and fights with white union men. Many newly arrived from the South soaked up the stories, their only source of information about unions. As they walked into their workplaces, they accepted the handbills Parker held out to them, warning them not to join the "White Man's Union." It all fit in nicely with the packers' goal to divide and conquer.

Keep blacks out was the mantra of the Chicago Real Estate Board as blacks continued to pour into the city and push the boundaries of the Black Belt into white neighborhoods. In April 1917, the Board appointed a committee of seven to orchestrate an all-out effort to keep blacks at bay. Take action now, they warned white homeowners, before property values fall.

Black leadership would have none of it. When the Real Estate Board tried to enlist the help of the *Defender*'s Robert Abbott and the Wabash YMCA's A. L. Jackson to persuade black realtors to keep hands off white neighborhoods, Abbott and Jackson turned them down flat. As reported in the *Chicago Daily News,* black leaders believed in black people's freedom to spend their money "wherever the white man's money is good."

On July 1, someone resorted to a violent approach, exploding a bomb in the hallway of a black family's home and blowing the front wall to smithereens. Police were on the scene quickly but did not find any leads. No arrests were made.

Summer moved into full swing and so did the meatpacking workers' union, the Stockyards Labor Council. This time, the union set up locals for unskilled workers throughout the laborers'

neighborhoods. An unskilled worker could join the local of his choice, but as union leaders expected, members sorted themselves along ethnic lines. With high hopes, the leaders established Local 651 in the Black Belt.

In September, the union was ready to sign up the masses. Leaders organized parades through the neighborhoods and meetings at union halls and in smoking rooms. On the street, organizers handed out fifty thousand flyers in various languages, all encouraging union membership: "BE MEN—JOIN THE UNION." John Kikulski was particularly effective, speaking in Polish and Lithuanian to capture the hearts of the eastern European workers. His predominantly Polish and Lithuanian Local 554 was the largest in the city.

This black family home was destroyed by a bomb.

Special efforts were made to reach out to black laborers, who were now a quarter of the Yard's work force and without whom the union was going nowhere. Reaching the old settlers was not difficult. Many in this small group of old-timers signed on. But the majority of black workers were migrants. This southern group, pleased with the wages and social perks courtesy of Louis Swift and other employers, was a tougher nut to crack.

Even so, the union was picking up enough steam to worry the government. President Wilson needed a steady production of meat from the Stock Yard to feed the hungry troops. A workers' strike could cut off food supplies, jeopardizing the war effort. Wilson was not about to let that happen. He took charge, stripping away the right to strike and appointing Judge Samuel Alschuler as federal administrator to arbitrate all disputes between the packers and the union.

In February 1918, the union organized the people of Packingtown to tell their story to Judge Alschuler. Referring to a novel published in 1906 about Packingtown's crumbling, disease-ridden community, union leader William Z. Foster commented, "It was as if the characters in *The Jungle,* quickened to life, had come to tell their story from the witness chair." Union lawyers highlighted the inequities of the laborers' lot by putting Louis Swift and other packinghouse owners on the witness stand to describe their own luxurious homes and lifestyles.

A month later Judge Alschuler issued his first order. Forty thousand men and women gathered in Davis Square Park in Packingtown to hear union leaders triumphantly announce the judge's decision to give packinghouse workers large wage increases and extra pay for overtime worked beyond an eight-hour day. Union leader John Fitzpatrick capitalized on the emotions of the moment to bring more workers—especially black workers—into the union fold: "It's a new day, and out in God's sunshine, you men and you women, Black and white, have not only an eight-hour day, but you are on an equality."

Now there was a flurry of registration for union membership. A white union leader gushed that organizers "do nothing but take in applications from morning to midnight." But a black union leader took a dimmer view: "The work of organizing [black laborers] has proceeded more slowly than I anticipated."

Down on the shop floor, it was clear that all was not well. Immigrants' distrust and anger toward the black race that had exploded in the 1904 meatpacking strike was still raging in 1918. Incensed immigrant workers lashed out at blacks with racial taunts. In one plant, someone hung a sign on the break-room door claiming the space "For White People Only." Blacks responded with profanities and ethnic slurs. Sometimes exchanges ended with threats of violence.

Summer brought these tensions outdoors. The warm weather had Chicagoans looking for fun at the parks and beaches. But there was not enough park space for all of the new residents crammed into the Black Belt. Some blacks started looking beyond their neighborhood for places to play in nearby white areas. The prospect of sharing space did not sit well with many whites.

At venues where blacks regularly outnumbered whites, facilities were unofficially redesignated for black use. Such was the case with the Twenty-Sixth Street beach. The head of the Municipal Bureau explained, "As the colored population gradually got heavier and more demand came for the use of that beach it gradually developed into a beach that was used almost exclusively by Negroes." At parks that remained mostly white, blacks were seen as intruders and fights were frequent. One park director recounted "some very serious clashes between the black and white children."

Migrants continued to pour into the city. Throughout 1918, property owners' associations stepped up their rhetoric to stop the "invasion." In October, a defiant letter sent out to white residents

The bleak area shown here was the largest playground in the Black Belt.

proclaimed: "We are a red blood organization who say openly, we won't be driven out." Physical violence was rising. Mobs frequently assembled outside the homes of black families who had ventured beyond the Black Belt, smashing up the buildings with bats, rocks, and bricks. Most frightening of all, between March 1918 and the end of the year, eleven bombs were exploded at the offices of black real estate agents and in the homes of black families.

A typical schoolyard playground in a white neighborhood, with plenty of equipment and children at play.

There was more to come. On November 11, 1918, the war ended. Soldiers began flooding back into the tension-filled city. Big Bill Thompson showed up to help celebrate the return of the all-black Eighth Regiment. But before long, the party was over and grim reality set in.

SIXTEEN
LAST STRAWS

As residents rang in the new year of 1919, there was plenty of anxiety to go around. Everyone worried about a shortage of jobs. Blacks worried the most. Past experience taught them that blacks were last hired, first fired, especially true for black women. One honest employer confirmed the truth in these worries: blacks were hired "solely on account of the shortage of labor. . . . As soon as the situation clears itself no more colored help will be employed." A black administrator for the United States Employment Service echoed the concern: "There has not been a single vacant job in Chicago for a colored man."

Black soldiers took it hard. They had risked their lives for their country, had fought with extraordinary bravery, were covered with medals of honor—the Médaille militaire, the Croix de Guerre, and the Distinguished Service Cross—heaped upon them by both the French and the Americans. Now, back at home, they were once more treated as unequal and unworthy of respect. One soldier bitterly observed, "I went to war, served eight months in France; I was married, but I didn't claim exemption. I wanted to go, but I might as well have stayed here for all the good it has done me." Yet this same soldier had gained a new resolve to persevere. Retracting his earlier thought, he concluded, "No, that ain't so, I'm glad I went. I done my part and I'm going to fight right here till Uncle Sam does his."

The soldiers of the Eighth Regiment returning from war, 1919.

Two bombs exploded in January 1919, both on the doorsteps of real estate offices, one black, one white. No arrests were made.

In mid-February, Judge Alschuler provided a bright moment for those who had the good fortune to be holding jobs in the packinghouses. His second set of awards gave out more wage increases and benefits. Still, white union workers were sour. They appreciated the extra money in their pockets, but they could not let go of the anger they harbored toward those men who reaped the same benefits but refused to join the union. And in their minds, nonunion and black were one and the same.

Black leaders were keenly aware of white Chicago's postwar desire to return to the days of blacks being nearly invisible in the overall fabric of the city. But there was no going back. In mid-March, A. L. Jackson explained to a group of white businessmen the new mindset of the returned black soldier: "[He] is coming back with a consciousness of power hitherto unrealized, a sense of manhood, and a belief in his ability to carry responsibility. He believes that his strength is the same as that of other men." And more darkly, he warned: "Young men among the negroes . . . are growing up with a suspicion against anything that is white."

In March, the banker and real estate mogul Jesse Binga was the target of two bombs, one at his real estate office, one at a property on his listings. No arrests were made.

In April, the battle of wills continued in the contest for the mayor's seat. Big Bill Thompson was running in a tight race for reelection. He had star status in the Black Belt, where Democrats were remembered as the party of the slave-owning southern planters, and Republicans as the freedom fighters. As far as black voters were concerned, Big Bill himself was still the best the Republican Party had to offer—always ready to take a public stand with them against those who would push them to the bottom.

Big Bill also had a lot of enemies. The Irish were incensed by his openly anti-Catholic propaganda. They were also threatened by his dedication to black causes to the detriment of their own. After his first victory in 1915, Thompson had appointed the black alderman Louis B. Anderson to be his floor leader in the city legislature. Anderson used his power to earmark municipal funds to clean up the Black Belt's crumbling sewers and streets. He also conducted an investigation of the police department, shining a light on racial discrimination and trumped-up criminal charges against blacks.

Three candidates crowded the field looking to unseat Big Bill. Robert Sweitzer was a dyed-in-the-wool Catholic Democrat, brother-in-law to a powerful Democratic ward politician. Middle-class progressives, disgusted by the corrupt politics of both Thompson and Sweitzer, threw their weight behind an independent reformer. A fourth candidate, supported by the Poles and Lithuanians, was put up by the Labor Party.

Robert Sweitzer and his wife cast their votes.

The race was heated, with candidates on all sides taking potshots. Approaching election day, Thompson and Sweitzer were running even, the race too close to call. Ragen's Colts and other athletic clubs pulled out all the stops for the Democrat, getting out the immigrant vote. On the other side, blacks like Mr. Horton showed their passion for the power of the ballot and came out in large numbers for Big Bill.

By the end of election night, it was clear that although he had garnered less than 38 percent of the vote, Thompson had been elected. It was also clear that without solid black support, he would have lost. In the communities of Packingtown, word went out that the blacks had won. The Democratic *Chicago Daily Journal* headline read "Negroes Elect Big Bill." There were still plenty of Democratic aldermen and department heads in city government. But they would now be in competition with the black agenda put forward by the two black aldermen and backed by the power of the Republican mayor.

In April, two bombs exploded, one at a real estate office, one at a private home. No arrests were made.

Employers were eliminating jobs no longer needed now that the war was over. Worker anxiety was at a fever pitch. In the month of May alone, unions across the nation battled with employers in 413 strikes and lockouts. The owners' access to strikebreakers was knocking the unions' teeth out.

Despite their victory at the polls, blacks continued to lose jobs to returning white veterans. The black work force in Chicago had fallen from sixty-five thousand in January to fifty thousand in May. The Wabash YMCA leader A. L. Jackson pleaded with Louis Swift and the other packers, disparaging returning immigrant soldiers, referring to them as "hyphenated"—Irish-Americans, German-Americans, and the like—and talking up native-born American black workers: "These [black] boys are all good Americans. There are no slackers, no hyphens among them." Yet black leaders were wary of being manipulated by these same packers. The *Defender* called them out: "Capital has not played square with us; it has used us as strikebreakers, then when the calm came turned us adrift."

Union leaders continued to press for unity, but they were talking against a tide of hate and mistrust. Whites wanted to force blacks to join the union. Blacks continued to resist. On the shop floor, fights broke out on a regular basis—barrages of racial and ethnic slurs, sometimes supported by guns and knives. Whites complained of black agitators who physically intimidated union organizers. One white union man accused a black laborer of threatening to split him open with a meat cleaver. Blacks complained of having bricks thrown at them. One man recalled, "Six or seven or eight Polocks [*sic*] grabbed a colored fellow out there . . . and said, 'you son-of-a-bitch, you will join the union,' . . . and one had him by this arm, and the other by this arm, and one fellow had him by the neck."

The housing shortage continued to grow, compelling more families to push into new neighborhoods. On May 5, a property owners' association convened a raucous meeting, exhorting white residents to hold the line against the threatening wave moving toward them out of the Black Belt. Statement upon statement echoed the cry of one real estate agent, who challenged neighbors to "stand together block by block and prevent such invasion."

Four bombings followed. The home of a prominent black family named Harrison was one of the casualties. From the moment in March when the family moved in, there was trouble. Insults hurled at the new neighbors were a daily affair. But on May 16, things got worse. Mrs. Harrison was in charge while her husband was away on business when a black janitor passed along a tip: Word on the street was that neighbors were planning to bomb the Harrison house. The police seemed uninterested, so Mrs. Harrison decided to protect herself. Her private security guard was

A poster warns whites about the consequences of voting for Bill Thompson.

checking the rear the following night when an explosion ripped through her front door and window. No one owned up to seeing anything. Now taking her more seriously, police were dispatched to keep watch. The following night, another bomb was thrown onto the Harrisons' roof from the vacant apartment next door. Someone had unlocked the door for the bomber. The police failed to question anyone. No arrests were made.

On this issue, Big Bill Thompson was no help. Twice, a delegation of black ministers tried to file a complaint about the bombings but was not allowed to see the mayor. The *Defender* reflected frustrations in the community: "The value of human life is cheaply held in these turbulent times . . . and the authorities constituted to preserve law and order seem helpless to cope with the situation. Chicago . . . is having a reign of this terror."

That spring and summer, once again the pattern of conflict spilled over into the parks and beaches. Blacks who tried to swim in white areas were turned away by white bathers and beach policemen; in parks, blacks were pelted with rocks.

The union continued to preach unity. In early June, John Kikulski spoke to an interracial group, saying, "Polish, Irish, Lithuanian, and in fact every race, color, creed, and nationality is to be included. . . . While there will be varied differences in our physical makeup and thoughts, there is one thing which we all hold in common, and that is our right to a living wage, and our rights in the pursuit of happiness as American citizens."

John Kikulski.

Throughout the month of June, the union wooed workers, setting up a band on a flatbed outside the Great Gate of the Union Stock Yard, greeting workers with lively tunes. As laborers started the trek home, union organizers—white and black—stood ready to sling a friendly arm around each worker's shoulders and lead him toward a line of trucks set up to whisk workers to union headquarters to sign up and pin on a button that read "100% Union or Bust!" The union used its newspaper, the *New Majority*, to foster goodwill between the Irish and blacks, where friction was the greatest. One edition highlighted a black-initiated petition calling on President Wilson to give Ireland a voice in determining international policy on postwar issues.

In the neighborhoods, white and black gangs were facing off with greater frequency. On June 15, boys scuffled in Washington Park, the large leafy park closest to both Packingtown and the Black Belt. Six days later, police came running to the park on a tip that the white gangs were out to kill all the blacks, but at the last minute, the gangs had dispersed and were roaming the city in smaller packs. By the end of the night, two black men were dead. The first was shot and killed minutes before midnight, a man in the wrong place at the wrong time. A bystander was able to grab the perpetrator and call for police, but when police arrived to find the assailant still standing there, revolver in hand, they let him go. The *Defender* headline screamed, "Ragan's [*sic*] Colts Start Riot."

A week later on June 30, two black brothers were chased off a streetcar and run down; one lived, one died. Days later, flyers flapped on posts in the Black Belt threatening to "get all the niggers on July 4th."

The Fourth of July passed quietly. The *Defender* commented, "NO 'RACE RIOTS' on the Fourth of July, what do you know about that?" But hysteria had taken hold. Reverend Carey preached to black worshipers in several black churches: "Be ye also ready." Terrified blacks began to carry knives for self-protection.

Meanwhile, the union was making some progress. Black Local 651 showed more than six thousand active members. A black organizer was optimistic. The union paper reported that he "was singing the blues a few days ago, but now he has a smile so broad that it is almost impossible to believe that such a change could come over a man."

Louis Swift and the other packers pressed hard to keep the workers from coming together. Using their clout with the downtown police department, they posted three hundred mounted police in the Stock Yard to break up union gatherings.

The union planned a culminating interracial parade for July 6. Leaders envisioned a powerful show of unity, a massive crowd of blacks and whites together parading through the Black Belt, crossing as one over the deadline, celebrating their common bond as laborers. The packinghouse owners pulled out all the stops to shut them down. Complaining to police of potential violence once more, the packers were successful in having the parade permit denied. Union leaders were not to be completely shut down, but the union was forced to scale back its plans, with separate parades for blacks and whites. The parades ended by converging in the park across the street from the Yard.

The interracial crowd exuded optimism. Many carried printed signs that read, "The bosses think because we are of different colors and different nationalities that we should fight each other. We're going to fool them and fight for a common cause—a square deal for all." Union and community leaders, four white and three black, gave emotional speeches glorifying the strength of a united laboring class. John Kikulski spoke in Polish, calling for "cooperation between blacks and whites." The *Defender* did not participate. T. Arnold Hill spoke in support of the union, but cautioned that the Urban League's expectation was that the union would not play favorites between the races.

The event was a success. But just two days later, the good feelings evaporated when immigrant workers at the nearby Argo corn refinery walked out and six hundred black nonunion men marched in to take their places. White packinghouse workers in Chicago felt a bond with the Argo immigrants. The strikebreakers at Argo confirmed in the immigrants' minds that nothing had

John Fitzpatrick addresses a large crowd of packinghouse workers.

changed, that blacks could not be trusted. On Friday, July 18, ten thousand packinghouse workers expressed their dissatisfaction by walking off the job. No more waiting for blacks to sign up with the union. The time was now. The men voted to submit demands for increased wages and benefits to the packers on Saturday, July 26, and, barring a satisfactory response, to go out on strike on July 28.

The threat was never acted upon. On Sunday, July 27, the storm that had been building for so long blew the city apart.

SEVENTEEN

RACE RIOT

WHEN JOHN TURNER HARRIS and his friends left the beach that Sunday afternoon in 1919, they were focused on the tragic death of Eugene Williams. They could not have imagined what would follow.

Back at the lakefront, black bathers stormed from Twenty-Sixth Street to the Twenty-Ninth Street beach. Spotting Officer Callahan, they shouted out for him to arrest Eugene's murderer, whose name turned out to be George Stauber. Ignoring them, Callahan turned to listen instead to a white man's complaint against a black man in the crowd. Adding insult to the blacks' injury, Callahan promptly arrested the black man.

A paddy wagon arrived at the beach to take the black man into custody. The swelling crowd jeered and threw bricks and rocks, and another black man in the crowd, James Crawford, drew a gun and fired it into a group of policemen. A black officer returned fire, bringing Crawford down. And just like that, the crowd entered into an unspoken agreement that guns were fair fighting.

People began to peel off in groups, making their way home. There were clashes between the races along the way. Rumors flew ahead of them, back to the neighborhoods. Around white neighborhoods the story went that the drowned boy was white and the stone thrower was black. In black areas, among stories of Officer Callahan's villainy was the claim that he had prevented expert swimmers from saving Eugene, and that he had held a gun on black bathers while they were pelted with bricks and stones. People poured out of their homes and into the streets, massing together to get the low-down. What they heard made them see red.

Around nine o'clock, darkness set in with its inherent cloak of anonymity for the lawless. Out in the streets, the rush of unleashed anger was palpable. Ragen's Colts emptied their clubhouse gun racks and went looking for targets. Terror reigned until three

THIS BOY'S DEATH CAUSED RACE RIOT

Eugene Williams

It was the drowning of Eugene Williams, 3921 Prairie avenue, at the 29th street beach Sunday, July 27th, that caused the city to be thrown in a general uproar for several days.

Williams was knocked from a raft by a rock said to have been thrown by George Stauber, a young white boy. Stauber is being held on a charge of murder.

Eugene Williams.

usual lightning speed, so that workers had no time to turn their thoughts or bodies to anything else. They worked side by side as always, Irish, Lithuanian, black. It seemed that the worst was over.

Those were their thoughts at the Great Gate. A few steps later, black workers saw the fate that awaited them. A little way down the road, a crowd of whites was assembled—men, women, children even—waiting in the heavy humid heat of the day, swiping hands across red faces to stanch the flow of sweat, white-knuckled fists clenched around the handles of switchblades and baseball bats. The mob included craftsmen and laborers, salesmen and trades-men, mothers and schoolchildren. But most were young men who belonged to gangs.

There was an instant when eyes met, when the danger became clear, when black minds frantically reached for an exit strategy. Someone in the waiting crowd shouted, "Get the niggers!" Then all hell broke loose. The mob surged forward. Black workers going home on foot ran helter-skelter down streets and alleys, ducking into doorways, jumping walls, crawling into cellars, the stampede of footsteps behind them. Some were lucky and gave

Blacks and whites board the streetcar at the end of a workday in the Union Stock Yard.

the mob the slip. Others were caught from behind, pulled from their hiding places, beaten, stabbed, and left to die. Here and there, a white man intervened on behalf of those being hunted down but quickly pulled back when the mob turned its vicious eye on the peacemaker.

Those blacks on streetcars may have thought they were safe as they pulled away from the Yard. But the crowd was not to be denied. Forming a human barrier, they stopped the streetcars in their tracks. A few young men, the leaders, showed off their physical prowess, detaching the cars from their wires. Those blacks on the streetcars now joined their brethren in the streets. Neighborhood police stood by and watched.

One of the black men under attack on a streetcar was relieved to see police coming to his rescue. But instead of expressing sympathy, one police officer yelled, "Come out of there, you big rusty brute, you. I ought to shoot you," and then smacked the man on the head, pushed him into the police wagon, and threw him into jail for a week, without allowing him to let his wife know he was alive. None of the attackers was arrested.

Arrival of the police after the stoning of a black man.

Back in the Black Belt, rumors of violence spread. Four thousand people gathered in the streets, becoming more and more agitated as news of the day circulated. An elderly Italian peddler on his way home for the evening, unaware of the rising emotions, wandered into the swirling mob. A gang of black boys pulled the man from his horse and cart, stabbed him to death, and left his body in the street. A white laundryman who worked a shop in the black community was later held up by three black men, robbed, stabbed, and left to die.

In the heart of the Black Belt, residents at the all-white Angelus apartment building were anxious. They could hear the hum of a disgruntled crowd rising from the street below. Blacks were gathering. The word on the street was that a white person at the Angelus had aimed a gun out of a fourth-floor window, downing a black boy walking below. The story spread and the crowd swelled. There looked to be a thousand angry black people milling around outside. As a black policeman recalled, blacks were pointing up at one window, shouting, "He shot from that window. . . . That is the window over there." Frantic, the tenants called for police protection that arrived in short order, a hundred uniformed men, some on foot, some sitting high on the backs of police horses. The crowd called for justice. The police searched the Angelus but returned empty-handed. This only made the people gathered outside angrier. It looked to them like another case of police refusal to arrest whites for attacking blacks. Out of the crowd, a brick flew. A policeman was hit. Officers returned fired, killing four, injuring many more.

People were panicked. Mayor Thompson mobilized the state militia, but the city's police chief did not want their help, and Mayor Thompson let him have his way. Six thousand militiamen were put on standby in nearby armories. All they could do was wait.

EIGHTEEN

RATCHETING UP

DAYLIGHT FADED TO DUSK and then to night. Many residents of the Black Belt were reluctant to retire into their stifling-hot homes, choosing instead the cooling breezes blowing across their front porches and steps. This proved to be a dangerous decision. Under cover of darkness, the gangs ratcheted up the action. Once again taking up the stashes of guns from their clubhouses, they piled into cars, revved up their engines, and sped across the deadline into the Black Belt. They tore up one street and down another, windows rolled down, guns pointed out, spraying bullets toward the darkened homes and anything that moved. From the shadows, shots rang out in response as black snipers took up position in yards, on porches, and behind windows.

At 8:30 p.m., a group of white toughs met up on a street corner. The plan was to take in a movie. A passing taxi driver leaned out of his cab window, alerting them to a group of rowdy white youths massing nearby, which sounded like a lot more fun to them. Abandoning the movie idea, they joined the mob in a night of roving violence.

At two a.m. they crossed paths with three couples walking together. Two of the men were lieutenants Washington and Browning, recently returned from military service overseas as members of the all-black Eighth Regiment. At this late hour, the officers would have preferred to take the streetcar, but at midnight, public transportation workers had followed through on a threat to walk out on strike, and so the officers were forced to make their way on foot. As they crossed Grand Boulevard, they heard a shout, "One, two, three, four, five, six," then a raucous cheer. The officers turned around and saw the toughs moving toward their group of six. A few came alongside while the rest got in front of them, cutting off any escape. Then they attacked.

For the soldiers, it was not an altogether unfamiliar experience, not unlike battle overseas—always having to be on the lookout for the enemy and ready to fight back to defend themselves. Now, here on Grand Boulevard, the soldiers responded to the attack. Gunshots rang out, and one of the white boys hit his mark, wounding Lieutenant Browning in his leg. Another of the young toughs lurched toward Lieutenant Washington, aiming to bring him down with an axe handle. But Lieutenant Washington was ready. He quickly drew a pocketknife, and as body met body, Lieutenant Washington drove the knife into his attacker, killing him. The mob moved on.

By night's end, 229 were injured and eighteen lay dead.

The morning light on Tuesday did nothing to slow the rioting. A pack of nearly one hundred young white men—many of them just returned from the war and proudly wearing their sailor and soldier uniforms—had pushed beyond the residential neighborhoods during the middle of the night and still roamed the city's downtown at daybreak. Marauding through railroad stations, bursting into hotels and restaurants, they smashed windows and tables, snatched up property that happened to catch their attention, looked for blacks to attack. Private security guards warned business owners of the danger to their property, urging them to get downtown to their stores and offices as quickly as possible, but the mob was not stopped until ten a.m. By that time, two more black men had lost their lives to the rioters' murderous attacks.

Most blacks did not go to work that day. With the streetcars down, the only way to get to the Stock Yard was on foot, and being out and about was just too dangerous. Only twenty-three of the twenty-five hundred blacks working for Louis Swift made their way to the Yard. Stranded at home in yet another day of oppressive heat, many took to the open air, sitting out on porches.

Blacks protected by police and militia bought provisions during the riot.

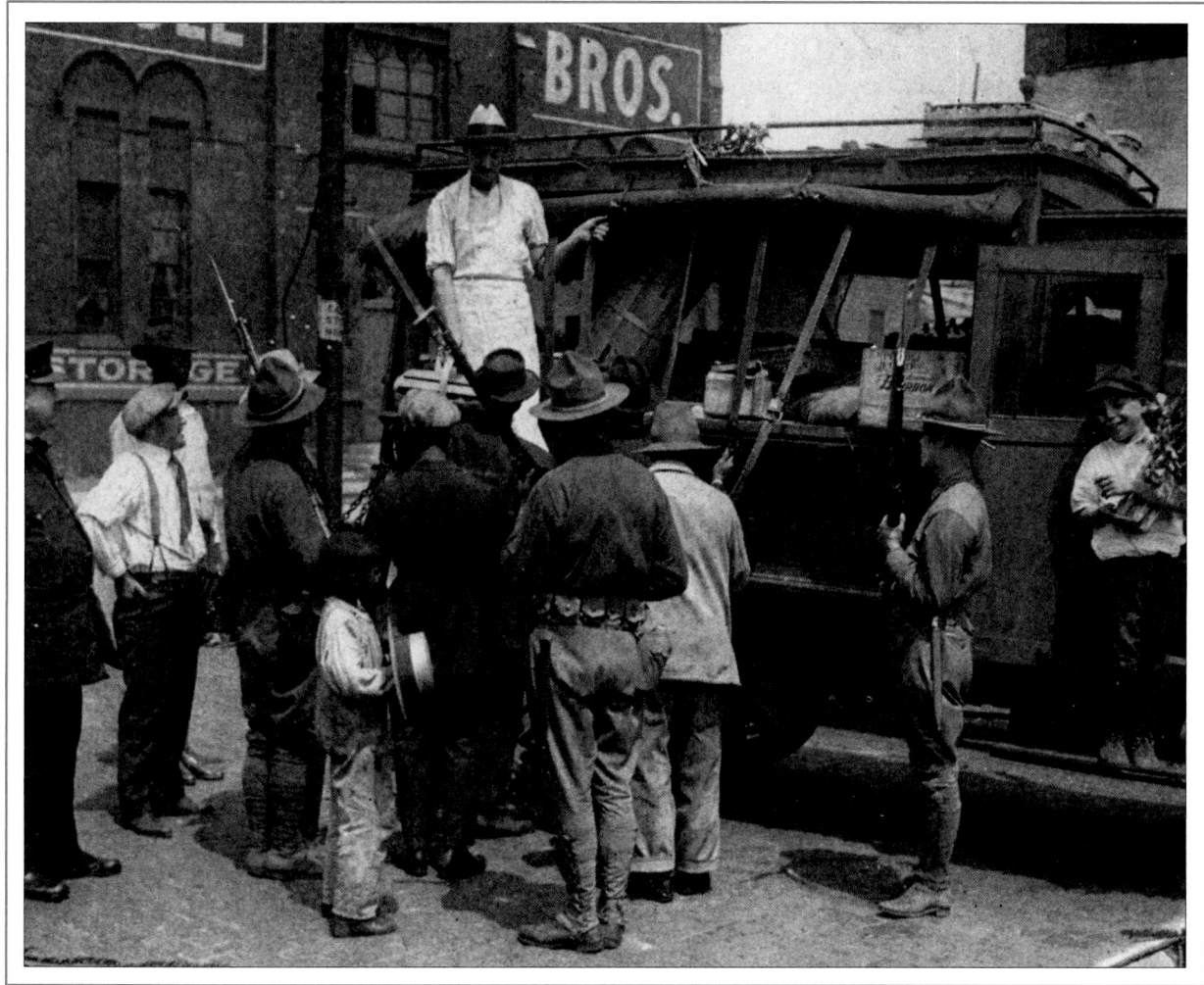

The *Chicago Tribune* reported that two-thirds of the dead were white. In truth, as the official riot report later verified, the numbers in the *Tribune* were reversed—two-thirds of those dead were black. The *Tribune* reported on the killing of a white woman and child. The *Defender* reported on the killing of a black woman and child. In fact, no women or children were killed. But the reports raised the panic level all around.

Without work, many blacks were dangerously close to running out of money for food. T. Arnold Hill led the Urban League's efforts to help, conducting a food survey and setting up a food station to distribute donated groceries. Churches contributed what they could. The union, still preaching peace and unity, also lent a hand.

The city's police chief stubbornly continued to resist assistance from the militia. The gangs continued to ignore his orders. They felt protected by their own.

As night fell, another round of car raids started up unchecked. Bullets sprayed the streets. A speeding car careened out of control, smashing into a police wagon. The cop, unharmed, exited his vehicle and walked toward the offender. As he came up alongside the reckless driver, a hand was thrust out of a passenger window flashing a police badge and ID. That ended the matter. Four-fifths of the entire police force was stationed in the Black Belt. No raiders were arrested.

By night's end, 139 more had been injured and eleven more lay dead.

NINETEEN

POINT-COUNTERPOINT

Wednesday morning, only sporadic outbursts punctuated quiet in the streets, but many were not convinced the trouble was over. Voices clamored for activation of the militia. Illinois's attorney general took a not-so-veiled swipe at Mayor Thompson, declaring, "I am convinced that these riots are the result of a plan carefully laid by a certain vicious Negro element which has been encouraged by a group of City Hall politicians." A Democratic alderman elected by the residents of Packingtown threatened escalated violence if the mayor did not take action: "We must defend ourselves if the city authorities won't protect us." Black leaders, including Ferdinand Barnett, concluded a two-day conference on the matter with a public statement calling on both the mayor and the governor to send in the soldiers. Louis Swift and the other packers added their voices, expressing frustration over the ineffectual government that was keeping black laborers away from work.

Bowing to the mounting pressure, Mayor Thompson toured the riot area. The quiet he beheld reinforced his belief in his decision to hold the militia at bay. Instead of bringing in soldiers, the police chief petitioned the city council for a supplemental cadre of special policeman.

Back in the Black Belt, living conditions were fast becoming desperate. Neither city nor business services had been able to get into the neighborhood while the uncontrolled violence was occurring. Garbage had not been picked up and was now overflowing in the streets. Grocery shelves were empty, grocers unable to restock. Church leaders and the *Chicago Defender* urged blacks to remain calm.

A wrecked house in the riot zone.

A new rumor was spreading: The gangs were hatching a plot to burn black families out. That evening, it started to look like the rumor was true. Rioting spilled over into previously white communities south of the Black Belt where blacks had recently been moving in. Roving these streets, gangs picked out the black homes, kicked in doors and smashed windows, then combed through the houses, ripping apart tables and chairs, tossing the broken shards of furniture into the streets, dropping oil-soaked rags to send them all up in flames. To a neighborhood white man who tried to intervene, the gangs spat out a warning: "If you open your mouth against 'Ragen's' we will not only burn your house down but we will 'do' you." Police did nothing.

Shortly before ten thirty p.m. on Wednesday night, the mayor reversed his decision. The nearly six thousand troops got orders to move out into the streets. As later recounted in a report on the riot, the commanders' instructions were simple and to the point: "They were to act as soldiers in a gentlemanly manner; they were furnished with arms to enable them to perform their duties; they were to use the arms only when necessary; they were to use bayonet and butt in preference to firing, but if the situation demanded shooting, they were not to hesitate to deliver an effective fire. Above all, the formation of mobs was to be prevented."

That night, a cool rain began to fall. Heated emotions simmered down. Violence took a brief rest.

On Thursday, some black laborers returned to work. But it turned out to be too soon. White workers in the Stock Yard still seethed with resentment and hatred toward the blacks they blamed for undermining the union. One white laborer struck a black man with a hammer. A mob of laborers then chased the black worker through some sheep pens, beating him with shovels and brooms until he keeled over dead.

Ida Wells-Barnett and the committee of black leaders were outraged at the absence of police protection. Ida reported on an

Police protection was provided for blacks removing their belongings from damaged buildings.

eyewitness statement that police "stepped aside" and "didn't raise a club" as they watched the attack in the Yard. She also condemned the discriminatory approach her committee observed being taken by police with respect to confiscation of arms: "Homes of white people are not searched but the constitutional right of citizens to bear arms is violated without compunction in the case of colored people."

In the Black Belt, there were signs of life returning to normal. Trucks were venturing back into the neighborhood, delivering a much-needed supply of fresh vegetables, milk, and ice. That evening, there was more reassuring news. The public transportation workers had voted to end their strike. Streetcars were to begin running at five o'clock on Friday morning.

As day dawned on Friday, streetcar service resumed. A communal sigh of relief was exhaled. Thousands of black packinghouse workers made their way across the streets of the Black Belt to the Urban League, the Wabash YMCA, and Jesse Binga's bank, where they stood patiently in line, exchanging the latest news, as they waited for distribution of emergency pay at stations set up by Swift and the other packers.

Blacks working on behalf of the company-sponsored Efficiency Clubs could be seen walking through the neighborhood, posting signs on trees declaring the riot to be over. The packers

Black packinghouse workers received emergency wages at the YMCA.

were promising security guards for protection on public transportation. The flyers urged blacks to return to work on Monday after a weekend of rest.

Union leaders were furious and scared at the same time: furious because the packers were making themselves out to be heroes to the black workers as the providers of both economic and physical security; scared because a return to work might be premature and disastrous. For months, even as they saw and heard the tensions and distrust on the shop floor and on the streets, union leaders had preached unity, urging blacks to trust them and their fellow Irish, Polish, and Lithuanian union men and women. They knew the seeds of goodwill had not yet taken root. They needed more time. And the riot had set them back; this they also knew. Just as surely, they knew that the men were still raw and not ready to make peace. A union representative tried to sway the packers: "These men will be on the killing floor of the packing plants. They will have cleavers and knives." Envisioning a bloodbath, he declared, "You must be insane to attempt such a thing."

The union leaders' plea fell on deaf ears. The packing company owners, the governor's staff, and the deputy chief of police met to put together a return-to-work plan for the twelve thousand black employees.

TWENTY

MOMENT OF TRUTH

AT 3:35 A.M. ON SATURDAY, an orange light burst into the inky black sky over the Lithuanian section of Packingtown. Sparks peppered the air. A thick gray smoke mushroomed up and slowly spread over the neighborhood rooftops and church steeples. Below, forty-nine frame homes were in flames. Nine hundred and forty-eight people were left homeless. A quarter million dollars of hard-earned money that had been invested in house and home was gone.

As people poured into the streets, rumors flew. A truck filled with black men had been seen near the site of the fires. An early milkman saw what he thought to be black figures coming out of a barn immediately before it burst into flames. But something about these stories didn't gel. When the milkman grabbed a nearby policeman to arrest the men, the policeman shrugged him off, saying he was "too busy" and "it is all right anyway." Firemen later confided to a Packingtown social services director, Mary McDowell, that there were no blacks involved. As the facts were pieced together, it appeared that the gangs were at work again, this time

Men surveying the burned-out Lithuanian community while the fire still smoldered.

smearing on blackface and burning out the Lithuanians in an effort to create a further appetite for vengeance against blacks—to keep the riot going.

With emotions running high, the packing company owners and the governor agreed that the potential for reignited violence was too great to risk throwing the races together. Union leaders welcomed the reprieve. It was safer for blacks to stay home. And the emergency pay they had received the previous day would keep them fed for another week. For now, blacks would not return to the Stock Yard.

Lithuanians wandered in shock through the rubble of their homes, finding the rumors hard to sift through. The *Tribune* was quick to report on witnesses who placed blame on blacks. The Lithuanians' fearless union leader, John Kikulski, pointed a finger at the packinghouse owners. The Polish newspaper accused the bosses of orchestrating the fires to further racial divisions among the workers. A popular Polish Catholic priest urged calm, calling the riots a "black pogrom" and hinting that the Irish were the culprits, trying to draw the Lithuanians into the battle. The union newspaper, the *New Majority,* pleaded for solidarity across racial lines: "Right now it is going to be decided whether the colored workers are to continue to come into the labor movement or whether they are going to feel that they have been abandoned by it and lose confidence in it."

Homes in the Lithuanian neighborhood destroyed by arson.

In the end, the Lithuanian community did not rise to the bait. Across Packingtown and the Black Belt, people returned to their homes. The streets emptied out except for the troops of the militia stationed to secure order. The last attempt to stir up trouble had been put to rest.

Sunday dawned cool and quiet. As John Turner Harris woke, it had been exactly one week since the fateful day at the beach—seven days of death and destruction as the city purged the rage that had been building for so long. Blacks would not return to work for another four days. The militia would remain on guard until the following weekend. But on this Sunday, the anger was spent. The city pulled back to lick its wounds.

EPILOGUE

In the Chicago riot, 38 people of both races died, all of them men; 537 more were wounded. Newspaper headlines around the country shone a light on Chicago's shame for all the world to see.

There had been other disturbances earlier that summer, in South Carolina, Texas, and Washington, D.C. The North was quick to label these outbreaks a southern problem; on July 23, the *New York Times* declared, "It could not have arisen in any Northern city." Just four days later, Chicago proved that judgment terribly wrong.

The troubles didn't end in Chicago, either. By the time the leaves turned color in the fall of 1919, America had experienced twenty-five riots, in large cities and small towns, from New York City to southern Arizona, an orgy of blood that would come to be called "Red Summer." The problems were not peculiar to Chicago. This was America's story. As one black minister commented, "It is not simply the shame of Chicago, but of the nation."

Some people felt blindsided. A white minister stated at a union meeting, "This riot has come to us as a shock after all our idealism." Others, like the editor of the *Defender,* were saddened but not surprised, judging that "those who believe . . . that the regrettable affair at the bathing beach here in Chicago was sufficient to set in motion this machine of destruction, are far from the right track."

The problems had been under the city's nose all along, if only it had chosen to address them. But before the riots, Chicago and cities across the country were focused on their successes—the money to be made, the technological innovations, the larger-than-life men and women, such as the Swifts, who stood tall as models of economic progress. Problems of the immigrant and black communities were swept under the dazzling carpet of success, where they grew until they forced their way into the open.

After the riot, Chicago had a choice. It could wash its hands of responsibility, placing blame on the poor. Or it could own up to its complicity. Some individuals took the narrow view, insisting that the culpability and the solution lay with the mobs. One man wrote a letter to the *Tribune* stating, "If the lawless insist on rioting, deal with them according to law, and we will soon be rid of them."

Chicago chose the braver path. Responding to a call by T.

An editorial cartoon in the Chicago Daily News *named the causes of the riot.*

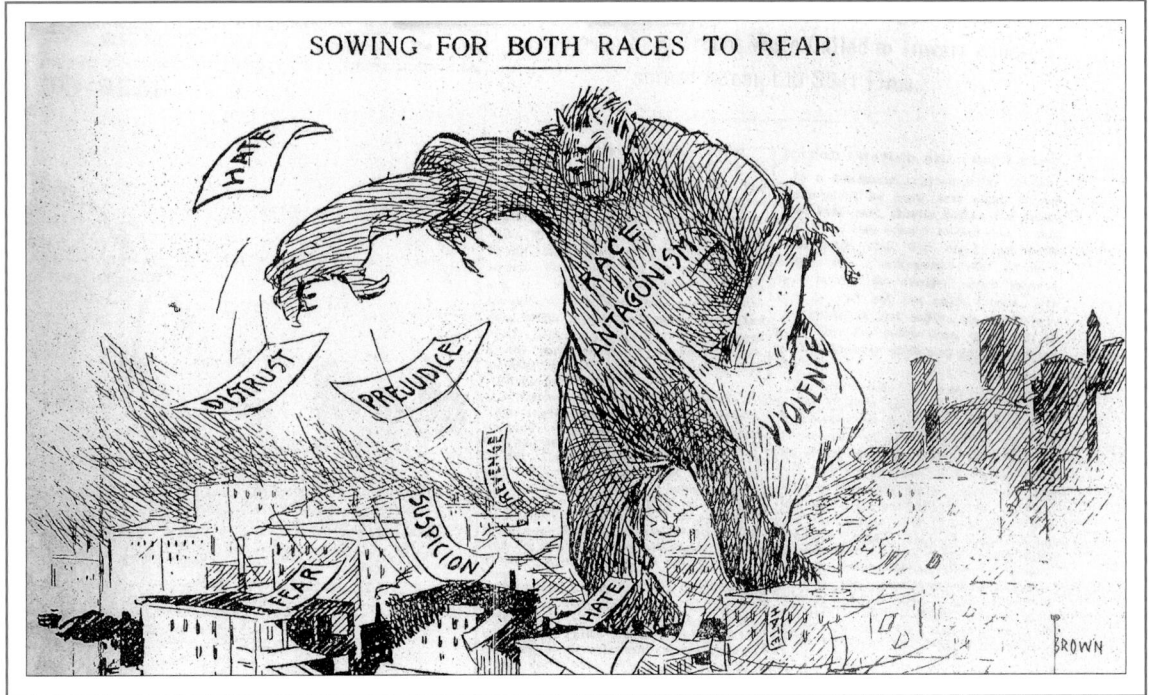

SOWING FOR BOTH RACES TO REAP.

Arnold Hill and other leaders of both races, a twelve-member commission—six blacks, six whites—was appointed to study the factors that led to the riot and to make recommendations for how to move the city forward. Charles S. Johnson, who interviewed Mississippi migrants in 1917, was a lead investigator for the commission.

The commission took its work seriously, reviewing records and talking with both well-known leaders and ordinary men and women. The final 651-page report detailed the causes of the riot and proposed a plan of action, calling on all Chicago citizens—police, government officials, employers, unions, churches, the press, and members of the public—to take ownership of the goal, so "that the civic conscience of the community should be aroused." The commission cautioned, "The remedy is necessarily slow." And it was. But some city leaders made an effort to step up in new ways.

The first task was bringing the rioters to justice. The city's actions in this regard were only partly successful.

Despite Officer Callahan's refusal to arrest him, George Stauber, the young man who threw the deadly rock that started the riot, was brought before the courts and tried for the intentional manslaughter of Eugene Williams. He was acquitted by a jury on May 27, 1920.

Officer Callahan was temporarily suspended from the police force but was soon allowed to return to his beat. He showed no remorse, telling the commission, "If a Negro should say one word back to me or should say a word to a white woman in the park, there is a crowd of young men of the district, mostly ex–service men, who would procure arms and fight shoulder to shoulder with me if trouble should come from the incident."

One hundred and twenty-eight indictments were brought for the beatings, shootings, stabbings, and arson. But justice did not roll for blacks as it did for whites: two-thirds of the riot victims were black, but only one-third of those indicted were white.

The Chicago Defender *(August 30, 1919) questioned the integrity of the post-riot investigation. The cartoon shows Justice barred from the room where the investigators met.*

Predictions of another riot came fast and furious in 1919 and 1920—warnings to expect a bloodbath on Labor Day, on Halloween, on May Day. But no further riots occurred. The commission concluded, "People of both races acted with such courage and promptness as to end the trouble early." The powerful tide of emotion had receded.

Lake Michigan still washes onto the sand at both Twenty-Sixth Street and Twenty-Ninth Street. On a hot day, white and black children splash side by side in the cool waters. To the west, century-old mansions and apartment buildings of the Black Belt stand alongside modern townhouses and high-rises in the predominantly black neighborhood that the residents now proudly call Bronzeville. Though the Barnetts, Abbott, Jackson, and Hill are long gone, the *Defender,* the Urban League, the NAACP, and Quinn Chapel remain cornerstones of the community, still called home by both middle class and poor. A busy interstate road divides Bronzeville from the communities that were Packingtown. With the development of interstate highways in the 1950s, meatpacking and shipping could take place in plants located closer to the farms where livestock was raised. Swift & Company, along with the other big meatpackers, moved out of Chicago to locations south and west. But the Great Gate of the Union Stock Yard still stands, just down the road from well-kept old homes on streets that the Irish now share with Asian and Latino families.

In the century since the riot, progress has come in fits and starts. Fifty years of continued migration from the South increased blacks' political muscle on the local level. In some cases, blacks have forged alliances with whites and Latinos to elect black mayors, senators, and congressmen. If Robert Horton had been alive in 2008, he surely would have preserved for posterity his November 5 copy of the *Chicago Defender,* announcing Barack Obama's election as the first black president of the United States.

Blacks have slowly begun to climb the economic ladder. A few have become owners of large corporations, some have risen to top levels in Fortune 500 companies, and larger numbers work as midlevel managers.

Still, America's present echoes its past. As of this writing, today's disparity between rich and poor is as wide as the divide between Swift and his laborers one hundred years ago. Nearly one-quarter of America's city dwellers live in poverty. One percent of all Americans take home nearly twenty percent of all earnings.

Black America is the bleakest of all. Ten million black men and women are laboring long hours in unskilled jobs, earning barely enough to get by. Nearly one in ten blacks—twice the rate of whites—are out of work at this writing, scanning job boards, filling out online applications, and standing in line at modern-day shapeups, hoping to land a job. There are one million young men roaming the streets in gangs, following in the footsteps of Ragen's Colts, brandishing guns to protect their turf. Around a third of these gang members are black. Millions of black men, women, and children are beginning and ending their days in rundown, paint-peeling, pipes-leaking homes reminiscent of the old communities of Packingtown and the Black Belt. Black men can expect to die, on average, five years younger than white men.

Full-blown riots have been few and far between. After 1919, the next large-scale unrest exploded nearly a half century later, when blacks took to the streets in cities across the country during the civil rights movement. Another twenty years passed before anger and distrust ignited rioting in Los Angeles in 1992. Between explosions, frustration and despair simmer. As President Obama has reminded us, if we look closely we will see the "quiet riots" on "any street corner in Chicago or Baton Rouge or Hampton . . . born from the same place as the fires and the destruction . . . [that] happen when a sense of disconnect settles in and hope dissipates." In 2015, this disconnect was once again forced into the light of day as violence surged in the streets of Ferguson, Missouri, New York City, and Baltimore.

In 1919, the riot investigation commission concluded, "But for [white gangs] it is doubtful if the riot would have gone beyond the first clash." In riots that have followed, poor blacks have been the ones to explode. But the riots have a common cause, as named by the civil rights leader Dr. Martin Luther King Jr.: "A riot is the language of the unheard." Dr. King was equally clear that future riots are not inevitable: "Social justice and progress are the absolute guarantors of riot prevention."

Ida Wells-Barnett understood that "eternal vigilance is the price of liberty." She never stopped working for a better world. Now men, women, and children all around us continue to follow in her footsteps. As fires burned in Baltimore, a five-year-old black child worked with neighbors and volunteers, sweeping up the debris, a small beginning toward picking up the pieces of her community. A black pastor worked with white businessmen to plan rebuilding of a Baltimore community center destroyed in the riot. In Ferguson, Missouri, artists, black and white, came together to paint murals of hope on boarded-up businesses. In New York, Chicago, and all across America, successful adults share their knowledge about the work world with middle-and high-schoolers. Police officers volunteer to read to students in public schools. Students are creating films, plays, and poems and are engaging with one another online to share their anger and also their hopes and ideas for a better tomorrow.

The challenge remains deep and wide. Human attention spans are short. Carl Sandburg, who witnessed and wrote about Chicago's 1919 riot, penned a poem about the cycle of convulsion and complacency: "Sometimes I growl, shake myself and spatter a few red drops for history to remember. Then—I forget." As we, the people, move forward, the ghosts of the Chicago riot of 1919 and of the other riots across the nation in that Red Summer whisper in the streets, calling us all to remember.

I Am the People, the Mob

I am the people—the mob—the crowd—the mass.
Do you know that all the great work of the world is done
through me?
I am the workingman, the inventor, the maker of the world's
food and clothes.
I am the audience that witnesses history. The Napoleons come
from me and the Lincolns. They die. And then I send forth
more Napoleons and Lincolns.
I am the seed ground. I am a prairie that will stand for much
plowing.
Terrible storms pass over me. I forget. The best of me is sucked
out and wasted. I forget. Everything but Death comes to me
and makes me work and give up what I have. And I forget.
Sometimes I growl, shake myself and spatter a few red drops for
history to remember. Then—I forget.
When I, the People, learn to remember, when I, the People, use
the lessons of yesterday and no longer forget who robbed me
last year, who played me for a fool—then there will be no
speaker in all the world say the name: "The People," with any
fleck of a sneer in his voice or any far-off smile of derision.
The mob—the crowd—the mass—will arrive then.

—Carl Sandburg

NOTES

There are many great sources of information on the economic, social, and political history of Chicago that ultimately exploded in the 1919 riot. Among these, there are several works that were instrumental in my broader research of the history leading up to the riot. Reference to these works is abbreviated as follows.

ABBREVIATIONS

WCJ   James R. Barrett, *Work and Community in the Jungle: Chicago's Packinghouse Workers, 1894–1922* (Urbana: University of Illinois Press, 1987).

IW   James R. Barrett, *The Irish Way: Becoming American in the Multiethnic City* (New York: Penguin Press, 2012).

NIC   Chicago Commission on Race Relations, *The Negro in Chicago* (Chicago: University of Chicago Press, 1922).

FB   Margaret Garb, *Freedom's Ballot* (Chicago: University of Chicago Press, 2014).

LH   James R. Grossman, *Land of Hope* (Chicago: University of Chicago Press, 1989).

AK   Anatanas Kaztauskis, "From Lithuania to the Chicago Stockyards—An Autobiography," recorded by Ernest Poole, *Official Journal, Amalgamated Meat Cutters and Butcher Workmen of North America* 5 (September 1904).

BC   Christopher Robert Reed, *Black Chicago's First Century*, vol. 1, *1833–1900* (Columbia: University of Missouri Press, 2005).

YY   Louis Franklin Swift and Arthur Van Vlissingen, Jr., *The Yankee of the Yards: The Biography of Gustavus Franklin Swift* (Chicago: A. W. Shaw, 1927).

RR   William M. Tuttle, *Race Riot: Chicago in the Red Summer of 1919* (New York: Atheneum, 1970).

IBW   Ida B. Wells, *Crusade for Justice: The Autobiography of Ida B. Wells* (Chicago: University of Chicago Press, 1970).

CHAPTER 1: THE BEACH

6   "KEEP COOL! . . . Beaches Today": Chicago Tribune, July 27, 1919.

7   "the bathing point of the south side": *Chicago Defender,* July 5, 1919.

        "As long as the raft was there, we were safe": *RR,* 5 (from Tuttle interview with John Harris, 1969).

11   "One fellow . . . we would duck": *RR,* 6 (from Tuttle interview with John Harris, 1969).

        stone meeting forehead: The coroner's report did not note any bruises on Eugene Williams's forehead. However, newspapers and the 1920 report of the Chicago Commission on Race Relations corroborate John Harris's recollections on this point.

        "I shook . . . blood coming up": *RR,* 6–7 (from Tuttle interview with John Harris, 1969).

        "Oh, my God": *RR,* 7 (from Tuttle interview with John Harris, 1969).

CHAPTER 2: A TIME TO REAP

12   "I wasn't . . . cool myself down": *RR,* 8 (from Tuttle interview with John Harris, 1969).

13   "For years . . . whirlwind": *Chicago Defender,* August 2, 1919.

CHAPTER 3: FREEDOM FIGHT

19 "but they . . . the community": *BC*, 93.

"'Mrs. Jones . . . 'Yes'": Blanchard, *Discovery and Conquests of the Northwest, with the History of Chicago*, volume 2, 301.

20 "content with . . . settled on him": *BC*, 73.

22 "revolting to . . . from oppression": Karamanski and McMahon, *Civil War Chicago*, 18.

23 "As there are times . . . self-protection": *Chicago Daily Journal*, October 3, 1850.

24 "Give us liberty . . . death": *Chicago Daily Journal*, October 3, 1850.

25 "great party of freedom": *FB*, 42.

CHAPTER 4: SELF-RELIANCE

27 "We are . . . free men": *FB*, 50.

27–28 "the people . . . helpful way": *IBW*, 23.

28 "Princess of the Press": *IBW*, 33.

"happy . . . living out of it": *IBW*, 47.

"The lynching . . . life": *IBW*, 47.

"an excuse . . . property": *IBW*, 64.

"punished with death": *IBW*, 62.

"She has . . . steel trap": *IBW*, 33.

"I, too . . . affairs": *IBW*, 228.

28–29 "The interest . . . church door": *IBW*, 241.

29 "continued warfare for our rights": McMurry, *To Keep the Waters Troubled*, 236.

29–30 "the Refined," "the Riffraff," and "the Respectables": Drake and Cayton, *Black Metropolis*, 48.

30 "Economically Dispossessed": *BC*, 284.

32 "incompetent": *Chicago Tribune*, May 6, 1903.

33 "the duties . . . in themselves": *IBW*, 249.

"the story . . . Joliet prison": *IBW*, 303.

33   "ounce of prevention": *IBW*, 413.

34   "vote for . . . our race": *IBW*, 345.

          "alert as . . . the wall": *IBW*, 415.

CHAPTER 5: WHITE NEGROES

35   "pretty tough hole": *NIC*, 12.

36   "an Irishman . . . tie": Sowell, *Ethnic America*, 27.

36–37   "Our immediate . . . slavery": Thrasher, *The Gang*, 212 (quotes from a letter of an Irish president of an American school board).

37   "There's a curse . . . out of it": Hoobler, *The Irish American Family Album*, 26.

          "We saw in it all . . . race and religion": Thrasher, *The Gang*, 212 (quotes from a letter of an Irish president of an American school board).

          "The colleens . . . 'Paddies'": Hoobler, *The Irish American Family Album*, 56–57 (recollection of James Michael Curley).

          "No Irish Need Apply": Dolan, *The Irish Americans: A History*, 96.

          "white negroes" and "smoked Irish": Ignatiev, *How the Irish Became White*, 41.

          "My master . . . common Irishman": Ignatiev, *How the Irish Became White*, 42.

          "the most depraved . . . the community": *Chicago Tribune*, February 26, 1855.

39   "untold riches": Wade, *Chicago's Pride*, 11.

          "was alive . . . heart and brain": Karamanski, *Civil War Chicago*, 1.

          "Only Irish Need Apply": Wade, *Chicago's Pride*, 33.

CHAPTER 6: WASTE MATTERS

40   "had a highly skilled trade . . . high priced men": *Butcher Workman*, March 1932.

          "It was wonderful . . . butcher": *Butcher Workman*, March 1932.

41	"Gustavus Franklin Swift . . . ahead": *YY*, 8.
	"When a clerk . . . front door": *YY*, 92.
42	"Big Three": Miller, *City of the Century*, 116.
	"To my father . . . too much!": *YY*, 8.
43	"Now we use . . . grunt": *YY*, 12.
	"a man worth . . . eye on": *YY*, 114.
45	"We walked . . . at all": *AK*, 25.
	"I felt poor . . . very bad": *AK*, 25.
	"It was . . . look at it": *AK*, 26.
47	"One boy . . . walked on": *AK*, 26.
	"bad . . . hungry": *AK*, 26.
47–48	"If you need . . . keep pace": *WCJ*, 27.
48	"They get . . . us men": *AK*, 26.

CHAPTER 7: PARALLEL UNIVERSES

49	"Packingtown begins . . . slowest to understand": Poole, "The Meat Strike," 183.
52	"The Catholics . . . different languages": French, *Biographical History of the American Irish in Chicago*, 9.
	"All are unanimous . . . the Church": French, *Biographical History*, 9.
54	"Generally . . . an insult": *National Provisioner*, October 1, 1921.
	"We punish . . . helpless": *Labor Enquirer*, March 2, 1887.
	"The presence . . . home life": Bushnell, "Some Social Aspects of the Chicago Stock Yards," 305.
	"They get . . . excused": *Labor Enquirer*, April 9, 1887.
56	"bitter brooding mothers": *Labor Enquirer*, March 2, 1887.
58	"tomato fights . . . and raids": Thrasher, *The Gang*, 69.
	"the Canaryville school of gunmen": Thrasher, *The Gang*, 16, 406.
59.	"When the Ragens . . . know it": *Chicago Tribune*, July 30, 1919.
	"Irish confetti": *IW*, 17.
	"We intend . . . Look out": *RR*, 33.
60	"a force . . . stockyards district": *Chicago Tribune*, August 6, 1927.

64 "the popular promenade . . . classes": *Chicago Defender*, June 18, 1910.

"for a minute . . . the 'Problem'": *LH,* 132.

CHAPTER 8: A STONE'S THROW

67 "A man . . . interfere": *Chicago Tribune,* July 16, 1864.

"with the honor . . . member": *Official Journal, Amalgamated Meat Cutters and Butcher Workmen of North America* 2 (May 1903): 27.

68 "revolutionized the industry": *Chicago Tribune,* March 30, 1903.

"from the man . . . consumer": Brody, *The Butcher Workmen,* 29.

"Obey . . . country": Brody, *The Butcher Workmen,* 52.

71 "I got nothing . . . decent job": Cayton, *Long Old Road,* 101, 107–108.

72 "the arm of the Church . . . righteous cause": *WCJ,* 174.

75 "unmanly and without self-respect": *RR,* 113.

"Shall the standard . . . citizens": *Railroad Trainmen's Journal* 21 (1904): 769.

CHAPTER 9: A HIGHER CALL

79 "fight for . . . at last free": Wilson, *War Message to Congress.*

"Let us take notice . . . chance to die": *Chicago Defender,* April 21, 1917.

"Many indulge . . . America": *Norfolk Journal and Guide,* September 24, 1917, printed online at historymatters.gmu.edu/d/5054.

82 "There is no color . . . any other": *Chicago Defender,* September 8, 1917.

CHAPTER 10: THE NORTHERN FEVER

86 "Wages is so low . . . live": Scott, "More Letters of Negro Migrants of 1916–1918," 419.

"Negroes grab . . . fodder": Scott, *Negro Migration During the War,* 30.

87 "The only wise thing . . . farm": *Chicago Defender*, January 16, 1915.

88 "For the hardworking man . . . says come": *Chicago Defender*, February 24, 1917.

89–96 The stories of the migrants in this chapter were captured and recorded in written notes of interviews by Charles S. Johnson, "'We Tho[ugh]t State Street Would Be Heaven Itself'": Black Migrants Speak Out," *History Matters: The U.S. Survey Course on the Web*, George Mason University, historymatters.gmu.edu/d/5337.

CHAPTER 11: A REAL PLACE FOR NEGROES

97 "They arrived . . . unpreparedness": *IBW*, 371.

98 "completely lost . . . go": *NIC*, 99.

100 "I just held my breath . . . something": *NIC*, 99, 301.

 "all over the car": *NIC*, 301.

 "This is a real place for Negroes": *NIC*, 301.

 "South State Street . . . sinners": Hughes, *The Big Sea*, 33.

CHAPTER 12: A JOB, ANY JOB

102 "For seven previous years . . . laundry": Scott, "Letters of Negro Migrants of 1916–1918,"291.

 "clear information . . . position": Scott, "Letters of Negro Migrants of 1916–1918," 291.

 "I used to . . . do anything": Scott, "Letters of Negro Migrants of 1916–1918," 296.

103 "to fit . . . the workers": *LH*, 202.

 "in the worker's mind . . . efficient employee": *LH*, 200.

104 "burn" : *NIC*, 390.

 "I'm an expert . . . family": *NIC*, 386.

 "had to take whatever they paid you": *NIC*, 386.

 "an overseer always standing over you": *NIC*, 172.

106   "The packing houses . . . everything": Scott, *Negro Migration During the War*, 26.

"place . . . full of life": *NIC*, 99.

CHAPTER 13: FULL TO BURSTING

108   "Rent goes up . . . it": *NIC*, 178.

109   "invasion": *NIC*, 119.

"You people . . . society": *NIC*, 206; Sandburg, *The Chicago Race Riots, July, 1919*, 14.

"There's a Nigger! let's get him!": *NIC*, 481.

"moved four times . . . living quarters": *NIC*, 178.

CHAPTER 14: RESPECTABILITY AND RESPECT

110   "dust caps . . . bedroom shoes": *NIC*, 193.

"loud talking . . . in public places": *NIC*, 193.

"It is our duty . . . climbing": *Chicago Defender*, March 17, 1917.

111   "A Few Do and Don'ts": *Chicago Defender*, July 13, 1918.

111–12   "Half a Million Darkies from Dixie": *Chicago Tribune*, July 8, 1917.

112   "the more unfortunate . . . race": *Chicago Tribune*, July 8, 1917.

"The Negro Problem": *Chicago Tribune*, July 8, 1917; May 4, 1919.

"subnormal": *LH*, 251.

"retarded": *NIC*, 256.

"no sticking qualities": *NIC*, 270.

"the limit . . . mental ability": *NIC*, 270.

114   "the emotional tendency . . . kill": *NIC*, 441.

115   "Quit calling . . . Mister That": *Chicago Defender*, April 21, 1917.

"Treat them . . . AS A MAN": *Chicago Defender*, April 21, 1917.

"not to take anything from a white child": *NIC*, 251.

"the spectacular . . . Chicago": *Chicago Defender*, October 9, 1915.

CHAPTER 15: TENSIONS RISING

121   "When . . . break them": *YY*, 181.

122   "White Man's Union": *NIC*, 429.

      "wherever the white man's . . . good": Sandburg, *The Chicago Race Riots*, 13.

123   "BE MEN—JOIN THE UNION": *RR*, 126.

124   "It was as if . . . witness chair": *WCJ*, 199.

124–25   "It's a new day . . . equality": *WCJ*, 200.

125   "do nothing . . . midnight": *RR*, 127.

      "The work . . . anticipated": *RR*, 127.

      "For White People Only": *Chicago Defender*, September 14, 1918.

      "As the colored population . . . Negroes": *NIC*, 277.

      "some very serious clashes . . . children": *NIC*, 280.

126   "We are . . . driven out": *NIC*, 118.

CHAPTER 16: LAST STRAWS

128   "solely on account . . . employed": *LH*, 184–85.

      "There has not . . . colored man": *RR*, 131.

128–29   "I went to war . . . Uncle Sam does his": *NIC*, 481.

130   "[He] is coming back . . . other men": "Chicago's Negro Problem", 75.

      "Young men . . . is white": "Chicago's Negro Problem", 75.

132   "Negroes Elect Big Bill": *RR*, 202.

      "These [black] boys . . . among them": "Chicago's Negro Problem," 76.

133   "Capital . . . adrift": *Chicago Defender*, April 26, 1919.

      "Six or seven . . . neck": *RR*, 155.

      "stand together . . . invasion": *NIC*, 119.

134   "The value of human life . . . terror": *Chicago Defender*, May 31, 1919.

135   "Polish, Irish . . . citizens": *RR*, 134.

136   "100% Union or Bust!": *WCJ*, 204.

BIBLIOGRAPHY

NEWSPAPERS AND MAGAZINES

Atlantic Monthly

Butcher Workman. Issues from 1932–1933.

Chicago Daily Journal

Chicago Defender

Chicago Tribune

Labor Enquirer

National Provisioner

New York Times

Norfolk Journal and Guide

Official Journal. Amalgamated Meat Cutters and Butcher Workmen of North America. 1900–1908.

Railroad Trainmen's Journal

JOURNAL ARTICLES

Bushnell, Charles J. "Some Social Aspects of the Chicago Stock Yards. Chapter I. Industry at the Chicago Stock Yards." *American Journal of Sociology* 7.2 (1901): 145–70.

——. "Some Social Aspects of the Chicago Stock Yards. Chapter II. The Stock Yard Community at Chicago." *American Journal of Sociology* 7.3 (1901): 289–330.

——. "Some Social Aspects of the Chicago Stock Yards. Chapter III. The Relation of the Chicago Stock Yards to the Local Community." *American Journal of Sociology* 7.4 (1902): 433–74.

——. "Some Social Aspects of the Chicago Stock Yards. Chapter IV. Constructive Suggestions for the Promotion of Democracy in Industrial Communities as Represented at the Chicago Stock Yards." *American Journal of Sociology* 7.5 (1902): 687–702.

Carter, Heath W. "Making Peace with Jim Crow: Religious Leaders and the Chicago Race Riot of 1919." *Journal of Illinois History* 11 (Winter 2008).

"Chicago's Negro Problem," *The City Club Bulletin,* 12 (March 17, 1919).

Poole, Ernest. "The Meat Strike," *Independent* 57 (July 28, 1904): 179–84.

Scott, Emmett J. "Letters of Negro Migrants of 1916–1918." *Journal of Negro History* 4, no. 3 (July 1919): 290–96.

——. "More Letters of Negro Migrants of 1916–1918." *Journal of Negro History* 4, no. 4 (October 1919): 412–19.

"Some Chicagoans of Note." *Crisis* 10 (1915): 242.

ONLINE SOURCES

BlackDemographics.com. "Poverty in Black America." blackdemographics .com/households/poverty.

Black Enterprise. "2015 BE 100s: The Nation's Largest Black Businesses." www. blackenterprise.com/lists/be-100s-2015.

Economic Policy Institute. "Black Unemployment Rate Dips Below 10 Percent in 11 of 24 States Measured in Second Quarter" (August 4, 2015) www.epi.org/publication/black-unemployment-rate-dips-below-10-percent-in-11-of-24-states-measured-in-second-quarter.

FamilySearch. "World War I United States Military Records, 1917 to 1918." familysearch.org/learn/wiki/en/World_War_I_United_States_Military_Records,_1917_to_1918.

Friedman, Lauren F. "This Chart Showing the Gap Between Black and White Life Expectancy Should Be a National Embarrassment." *Business*

Insider, January 9, 2014. www.businessinsider.com/huge-racial-gap-in-life-expectancy-2014-1.

Gangsters Inc. "Puparo's Gangland History of the Chicago Boroughs." Published September 25, 2013. gangstersinc.ning.com/profiles/blogs/puparo-s-gangland-history-of-the-chicago-boroughs-1.

Gonzales, Nathan L. "Why Can't Latinos Get Elected to Latino Congressional Districts?" MSNBC.com. NBC News Digital, September 13, 2013. www.msnbc.com/msnbc/why-cant-latinos-get-elected-latino-congr.

Green, Erica L. "City Students Turn to Writing to Process Baltimore Unrest." *Baltimore Sun,* May 3, 2015. www.baltimoresun.com/news/maryland/education/bs-md-black-words-matter-20150503-story.html.

National Gang Center. "National Youth Gang Survey Analysis." 1996–2011. www.nationalgangcenter.gov/Survey-Analysis.

National Museum of the US Air Force. "Liberty 12-Cylinder." Published April 7, 2015. www.nationalmuseum.af.mil/Visit/MuseumExhibits/FactSheets/Display/tabid/509/Article/196760/liberty-12-cylinder.aspx.

Rockoff, Hugh. "U.S. Economy in World War I." In EH.Net Encyclopedia, edited by Robert Whaples. Published February 10, 2008. eh.net/encyclopedia/u-s-economy-in-world-war-i.

Sam Houston State University. "New Study Finds U.S. Juvenile Gang Membership Tops 1 Million." Published February 16, 2014. www.shsu.edu/pin_www/T@S/2015/gangstudy.html.

schooltube.com

Sifakis, Carl. *The Mafia Encyclopedia.* New York: Facts on File, 2005. militero.files.wordpress.com/2011/04/the-mafia-encyclopedia.pdf.

Statista: The Statistics Portal. "Percentage of People Who Live Below the Poverty Level in the Most Populated Cities in the U.S. in 2014." www.statista.com/statistics/205637/percentage-of-poor-people-in-the-top-20-most-populated-cities-in-the-us.

Statistical Atlas. "Race and Ethnicity in Bridgeport, Chicago, Illinois (Neighborhood)." statisticalatlas.com/neighborhood/Illinois/Chicago/Bridgeport/Race-and-Ethnicity.

Tax Foundation November 2015. taxfoundation.org/sites/taxfoundation.

org/files/docs/TF_FF491_Summary%20of%20the%20Latest%20
Federal%20Income%20Tax%20Data%2C_2015%20Update.pdf.

U.S. Bureau of Labor Statistics. *Characteristics of Minimum Wage Workers, 2013.* BLS
Reports. Report 1048. March 2014. www.bls.gov/cps/minwage2013.pdf.

U.S. Bureau of Labor Statistics. "Table A-2. Employment Status of the Civil-
ian Population by Race, Sex, and Age." Economic News Release. Updated
November 2015. www.bls.gov/news.release/empsit.t02.htm.

Wallace, Gregory. "Only 5 Black CEOs at 500 Biggest Companies."
CNN Money. Cable News Network, January 29, 2015. money.cnn.
com/2015/01/29/news/economy/mcdonalds-ceo-diversity.

Wood, Pamela. "Church, Developer Vow to Finish Senior Apartments
Destroyed by Fire." *Baltimore Sun,* May 4, 2015. www.baltimoresun.com/
news/maryland/baltimore-city/bs-md-mary-harvin-transformation-
center-20150504-story.html.

SPEECHES AND INTERVIEWS

Johnson, Charles S. "'We Tho[ugh]t State Street Would Be Heaven Itself'":
Black Migrants Speak Out. *History Matters: The U.S. Survey Course on the Web.*
George Mason University. historymatters.gmu.edu/d/5337.

King, Martin Luther, Jr. "The Other America." Stanford University. April
14, 1967.

Wilson, Woodrow. *War Message to Congress.* April 2, 1917. www.lib.byu.edu/
index.php/Wilson's_War_Message_to_Congress.

BOOKS

Abbot, Edith. *The Tenements of Chicago 1908–1935.* New York: Arno, 1970.

Barrett, James R. *The Irish Way: Becoming American in the Multiethnic City.* New York:
Penguin Press, 2012.

———. *Work and Community in the Jungle: Chicago's Packinghouse Workers, 1894–1922.*
Urbana: University of Illinois Press, 1987.

BIBLIOGRAPHY ~ 185

Blanchard, Rufus. *Discovery and Conquests of the North-west, with the History of Chicago, Volume 2.* Chicago: R. Blanchard and Company, 1900.

Brody, David. *The Butcher Workman: A Study of Unionization.* Cambridge, MA: Harvard University Press, 1964.

Bukowski, Douglas. *Big Bill Thompson, Chicago, and the Politics of Image.* Urbana: University of Illinois Press, 1998.

Cayton, Horace R. *Long Old Road.* New York: Trident Press, 1965.

Chicago Commission on Race Relations. *The Negro in Chicago.* Chicago: University of Chicago Press, 1922.

Deignan, Tom. *Irish Americans.* Reprint. Hauppauge, NY: Barron's Educational Series, 2003. Reprinted from UK: Ivy Press.

Diamond, Andrew J. *Mean Streets.* Oakland: University of California Press, 2009.

Dolan, Jay P. *The Irish Americans: A History.* New York: Bloomsbury Press, 2008.

Drake, St. Clair, and Horace R. Cayton. *Black Metropolis: A Study of Negro Life in a Northern City.* Rev. ed. 1970. Reprint, Chicago: University of Chicago Press, 1993.

Ford, Henry, and Samuel Crowther. *My Life and Work.* Garden City, NY: Doubleday, Page, 1922.

French, Charles, ed. *Biographical History of the American Irish in Chicago.* Chicago: American Biographical Pub., 1897.

Garb, Margaret. *Freedom's Ballot: African American Political Struggles in Chicago from Abolition to the Great Migration.* Chicago: University of Chicago Press, 2014.

Grossman, James R., Ann Durkin Keating, and Janice L. Reiff. *The Encyclopedia of Chicago.* Chicago: University of Chicago Press, 2004.

Grossman, James R. *Land of Hope: Chicago, Black Southerners, and the Great Migration.* Chicago: University of Chicago Press, 1989.

Halpern, Rick. *Down on the Killing Floor: Black and White Workers in Chicago's Packinghouses, 1904–54.* Urbana: University of Illinois Press, 1997.

Harpster, Jack. *The Railroad Tycoon Who Built Chicago: A Biography of William B. Ogden.* Carbondale: Southern Illinois University Press, 2009.

Herbst, Alma. *The Negro in the Slaughtering and Meat-Packing Industry in Chicago.* Boston and New York: Houghton Mifflin, 1932.

Hoobler, Dorothy, and Thomas Hoobler. *The Irish American Family Album.* New York: Oxford University Press, 1995.

Hughes, Langston. *The Big Sea: An Autobiography.* New York: Alfred A. Knopf, 1945.

Ignatiev, Noel. *How the Irish Became White.* New York: Routledge, 1995.

Karamanski, Theodore J., and Eileen M. McMahon, eds. *Civil War Chicago: Eyewitness to History.* Athens: Ohio University Press, 2014.

Klein, Carol Swartout, *Painting for Peace in Ferguson.* Saint Louis: Treehouse Publishing Group, 2015.

Krist, Gary. *City of Scoundrels: The 12 Days of Disaster That Gave Birth to Modern Chicago.* New York: Crown Publishers, 2012.

McCaffrey, Lawrence J. *The Irish in Chicago.* Urbana: University of Illinois Press, 1987.

McGreevy, John T. *Catholicism and American Freedom: A History.* New York: W. W. Norton, 2003.

McMurry, Linda O. *To Keep the Waters Troubled: The Life of Ida B. Wells.* New York: Oxford University Press, 1998.

McWhirter, Cameron. *Red Summer: The Summer of 1919 and the Awakening of Black America.* New York: Henry Holt, 2011.

Miller, Donald L. *City of the Century: The Epic of Chicago and the Making of America.* New York: Simon & Schuster, 1996.

Ottley, Roi. *The Lonely Warrior: The Life and Times of Robert S. Abbott, Founder of the* Chicago Defender. Chicago: H. Regnery, 1955.

Pacyga, Dominic A. *Chicago: A Biography.* Chicago: University of Chicago Press, 2009.

———. *Polish Immigrants and Industrial Chicago: Workers on the South Side, 1880–1922.* Columbus: Ohio State University Press, 1991.

———. *Slaughterhouse: Chicago's Union Stock Yard and the World It Made.* Chicago: University of Chicago Press, 2015.

Pierce, Bessie Louise. *A History of Chicago: The Beginning of a City, 1673–1848.* 1937. Reprint. Chicago: University of Chicago Press, 1970.

———. *A History of Chicago: From Town to City: 1848–1871.* 1940. Reprint. Chicago: University of Chicago Press, 1970.

———. *A History of Chicago: The Rise of a Modern City, 1871–1893.* 1957. Reprint. Chicago: University of Chicago Press, 1970.

Pierce, Bessie Louise, and Joe Lester Norris. *As Others See Chicago: Impressions of Visitors, 1673–1933.* Chicago: University of Chicago Press, 1933.

Reed, Christopher Robert. *Black Chicago's First Century.* Vol. 1, *1833–1900.* Columbia: University of Missouri Press, 2005.

Rossa, O'Donovan. *Rossa's Recollections.* Mariner's Harbor, NY: O'Donovan Rossa, 1898.

Sandburg, Carl. *The Chicago Race Riots, July, 1919.* New York: Harcourt, Brace and Howe, 1919.

———. *The Complete Poems of Carl Sandburg.* Revised and expanded ed. New York: Harcourt, Brace, 1970.

Scott, Emmett J. *Negro Migration During the War.* New York: Oxford University Press, 1920.

Slaughter, Thomas P. *Bloody Dawn: The Christiana Riot and Racial Violence in the Antebellum North.* New York: Oxford University Press, 1991.

Sowell, Thomas. *Ethnic America.* New York: Basic Books, 1981.

Spear, Allan H. *Black Chicago: The Making of a Negro Ghetto, 1890–1920.* Chicago: University of Chicago Press, 1967.

Swift, Helen. *My Father and My Mother.* Chicago: Printed privately, 1937.

Swift, Louis Franklin, and Arthur Van Vlissingen, Jr. *The Yankee of the Yards: The Biography of Gustavus Franklin Swift.* Chicago: A. W. Shaw, 1927.

Thrasher, Frederic M. *The Gang: A Study of 1,313 Gangs in Chicago.* 1927. 2nd ed. Chicago: University of Chicago Press, 1936.

Tuttle, William M., Jr. *Race Riot: Chicago in the Red Summer of 1919.* New York: Atheneum, 1970.

Wade, Louise Carroll. *Chicago's Pride: The Stockyards, Packingtown, and the Environs in the Nineteenth Century.* Urbana: University of Illinois Press, 1987.

Walsh, Margaret. *The Rise of the Midwestern Meat Packing Industry.* Lexington: University Press of Kentucky, 1982.

Washington, Booker T. *The Booker T. Washington Papers, Vol. 13: 1914–1915.* Edited by Louis R. Harlan and Raymond W. Smock. Urbana: University of Illinois Press, 1984.

Washington, Sylvia Hood. *Packing Them In: An Archaeology of Environmental Racism in Chicago, 1865–1954.* Lanham, MD: Lexington, 2005.

Wells, Ida B. *Crusade for Justice: The Autobiography of Ida B. Wells.* Chicago: University of Chicago Press, 1970.

PICTURE CREDITS

Chicago Daily News/Chicago History Museum/Getty Images: **14–15**.

Chicago Daily News/public domain: **162**.

Chicago History Museum: ICHi-06418, **134**; ICHi-091385, **66**; ICHi-12633, **42**; ICHi-15016, **69**; ICHi-21018, **53**; ICHi- 21355, **138–139**; ICHi-28567, **93**; ICHi-30315, **142**; ICHi-31736, **154**; ICHi-38004-A, **123**; ICHi-40220, **103**; ICHi-67641, **116**; ICHi-89265, **101**; ICHi-89266, **105**; ICHi-89267, **112**; ICHi-89268, **114**; ICHi- 89269, **126**; ICHi-89270, **127**; ICHi-89271, **144**; ICHi- 89272, **145**; ICHi-89273, **149**; ICHi-89274, **155**; ICHi-89275, **159**; ICHi-89276, **158**.

Chicago History Museum/Aaron E. Darling: ICHi-62485, **18**; ICHi-89277, **22**.

Chicago History Museum/Circuit Court of Madison Country (Ill.): ICHi-36297, **21**.

Chicago History Museum/Chicago Daily News Negatives Collection: DN-0000502, **56**; DN-0000716, **91**; DN-0000884, **73**; DN-0000889, **57**; DN-0000906, **70**; DN-0000923, **51**; DN-0000954, **74**; DN-0000967, **54**; DN-0001027, **48**; DN-0001520, **46**; DN-0006679, **31**; DN-0007198, **44**; DN-0061768, **59**; DN-0064311, **131**; DN-0069075, **81**; DN-0071295, **135**; DN-0071299, **152**; DN-0073280, **10**.

Chicago History Museum/Getty Images: **ii–iii**, **2–3**, **76–77**, **118–119**.

Chicago Public Library, Special Collections and Preservation Division, BNL 8.43/J. B. Wilson: **63**.

Chicago Tribune: **8–9** (July 27, 1919 © 1919 Chicago Tribune. All rights reserved. Used by permission and protected by the Copyright Laws of the United States. The printing, copying, redistribution, or retransmission of this Content without express written permission is prohibited), **13** (public domain), **129** (February 18, 1919 © 1919 Chicago Tribune. All rights reserved. Used by permission and protected by the Copyright Laws of the United States. The printing, copying, redistribution, or retransmission of this Content without express written permission is prohibited).

Courtesy of the Chicago Defender: **80, 83, 87, 88, 95, 141, 166**.

Courtesy of the University of Illinois at Chicago Library: **99** (Aldis Family Papers, box 1, folder 6, AFP_0001_0006_001a and AFP_0001_0006_001b, Special Collections), **24** (*The Negro in Chicago*).

The Crisis/public domain: **62**.

HarpWeek/Harper's Weekly Magazine: **38**.

HERB (herb.lw4.gc.cuny.edu): **108**.

Public domain: **164**.

University of Chicago Library, Special Collections Research Center: **27, 29**.

in, 84; 1904 strike against, 69–74, 125; opening of, 39, 41; pecking order in, 104; strikebreakers and, 69–73; unskilled immigrants in, 35, 45–47; women in, 68, 84; working conditions in, 47–49, 48

United States Employment Service, 128

Urban League, 98, 99, 100, 102–105, 108–III, IIO–III, 138, 150, 155

V

Voting rights, 33–34, 90

W

Wabash YMCA, 32, 64, 100, 104–105, II3, 122, 132, *155*, 155

Washington, Booker T., 93

Washington, D.C., race disturbances in, 161

Washington, Lt., 148

Washington Park, 136

Wells, Ida B., Club, 32–33

Wells-Barnett, Ida B., 27–29, 32–34, 63, 80, 85–86, 97, 100, II3, 143, 153–154, 165, 169

Williams, Charles, I, 5–7

Williams, Eugene, I, 5–7, 10– II, 13, 17, 18, 136, 140–141, 163, 164, 165

Williams, Lawrence, I, 5–7

Williams, Paul, I, 5–7

Wilson, Woodrow, 79, 80, 84, 124, 136

Wolves (black gang), 57

Women: in Black Belt, III; concerns of packinghouse employees, 68; in

Packingtown, 52, 55–57; in Union Stock Yard, 68, 84; voting rights for, 33

Women's clubs, 82

World War I, 10, 79–84, 86– 88, 121, 127